THE GR11 – LA SENDA

THROUGH THE SPANISH PYRENEES

About the Author

Since taking early retirement from his career as a physics and sports teacher, Brian Johnson has found time for three through-hikes of the Pacific Crest Trail, a 2700-mile round-Britain walk, four hikes across the Pyrenees from the Atlantic to the Mediterranean, a hike along the Via de la Plata from Seville to Santiago and a single summer compleation of the Munros (Scotland's 3000ft mountains) as well as climbing all the Corbetts (Scotland's 2500ft–3000ft mountains). He has also completed a 2200-mile cycle tour of Spain and France and done multi-week canoe tours in Sweden, France, Spain and Portugal.

In his younger days, Brian's main sport was orienteering. He competed at a high level and coached both Bishop Wordsworth's School and South-West Junior Orienteering Squads. He also surveyed and drew many orienteering maps. He has walked and climbed extensively in summer and winter conditions in Britain, the Alps, the Pyrenees and California, often leading school groups.

As a fanatical sportsman and games player, Brian competed to a high level in cricket, hockey, bridge and chess. His crowning achievement was winning the 1995/96 World Amateur Chess Championships.

Other Cicerone guides by the author
The Pacific Crest Trail
Walking the Corbetts Volume 1: South of the Great Glen
Walking the Corbetts Volume 2: North of the Great Glen

THE GR11 – LA SENDA

THROUGH THE SPANISH PYRENEES

by Brian Johnson

2 POLICE SQUARE, MILNTHORPE, CUMBRIA LA7 7PY
www.cicerone.co.uk

© Brian Johnson 2014
Fifth edition 2014
ISBN: 978 1 85284 725 8

Fourth edition 2008
Third edition 2004
Second edition 2000
First edition 1996
1 85284 524 7

Printed in China on behalf of Latitude Press Ltd
A catalogue record for this book is available from the British Library.
All photographs are by the author.

lovelljohns.com   Route mapping by Lovell Johns

Advice to Readers

While every effort is made by our authors to ensure the accuracy of guidebooks as they go to print, changes can occur during the lifetime of an edition. If we know of any, there will be an updates tab on this book's page on the Cicerone website (www.cicerone.co.uk), so please check before planning your trip. We also advise that you check information about such things as transport, accommodation and shops locally. We are always grateful for information about any discrepancies between a guidebook and the facts on the ground, sent by email to info@cicerone.co.uk or by post to Cicerone, 2 Police Square, Milnthorpe LA7 7PY, United Kingdom.

Front cover: Lac de Mar (Stage 22, recommended GR11-18 variation)

CONTENTS

Map Key

🚶	start of day's walk
🚶	end of day's walk
🚶	start/finish point
S	alternative start
F	alternative finish
——————	GR11 featured route
– – – – –	GR11 alternative route
··················	optional route
- - - - - - -	minor track or dirt road
- - - - - - -	minor track or path
▬▭▬▭▬	railway
●	railway station
○	settlement
■	significant building
▲	summit
⌂	accommodation
⌂	bothy (unmanned refuge)
⊗	campground
⊗	bar/restaurant
𝒊	tourist information office
🛒	food shop
W	water
⊼	picnic site
)(	saddle/col

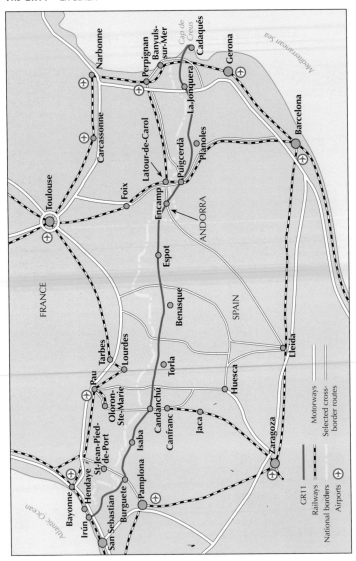

8

PUBLISHER'S DEDICATION

Punta Gabedallo over Ibón d'Estanés (Stage 10)

This new GR11 guide is dedicated to the memory of Paul Lucia.

Paul pioneered La Senda and the Spanish Pyrenees for English-speaking trekkers nearly 20 years ago. Paul's first edition came out in 1996 under the aegis of Walt Unsworth, my predecessor as Publisher at Cicerone. New updated editions that I worked on with Paul followed in 2000 and 2004, with a final posthumous edition in 2008, the proofs of which were checked by Paul's son P-J and daughter Anna.

Paul brought a lifetime's precision to his passion for the Spanish side of the Pyrenees, the result of which was a guide that Cicerone was proud to publish for many years. Many trekkers have commented that Paul had very long legs and his timings were referred to as 'bold' by some, unattainable by others! I particularly remember well Paul's frustration with the continual re-routing in Navarre, although he was delighted to have an excuse to return to the route.

In the 2008 edition, P-J and Anna wrote: 'If asked to describe our father, the word "indomitable" invariably springs to mind. Dad's exploits formed a thread of marvellous adventure through our upbringing.'

My thanks to Christine Lucia for agreeing to let us build on Paul's work, to Paul's family and the many Cicerone trekkers whose comments have helped the GR11 and our guides to it go from strength to strength.

Jonathan Williams, Milnthorpe, January 2014

Mountain Safety

Every mountain walk has its dangers, and those described in this guidebook are no exception. All who walk or climb in the mountains should recognise this and take responsibility for themselves and their companions along the way. The author and publisher have made every effort to ensure that the information contained in this guide was correct when it went to press, but they cannot accept responsibility for any loss, injury or inconvenience sustained by any person using this book.

International Distress Signal *(emergency only)*
Six blasts on a whistle (and flashes with a torch after dark) spaced evenly for one minute, followed by a minute's pause. Repeat until an answer is received. The response is three signals per minute followed by a minute's pause.

Helicopter Rescue
The following signals are used to communicate with a helicopter:

Help needed:
raise both arms
above head to
form a 'Y'

Help not needed:
raise one arm
above head, extend
other arm downward

Emergency telephone numbers
Spain: The Guardia Civil (police) are responsible for mountain rescue in Spain. Tel 112.
Andorra and France: Mountain rescue tel 112.

AUTHOR'S PREFACE

Limestone outcrops, Sierra de Abodi (Stage 6)

The first Cicerone guide to the GR11 was published in 1996. At that time the route was ill-defined with little waymarking; navigation was a serious problem and there was much walking on tarmac and dirt roads. Constant changes and improvements in the route kept Paul Lucia busy producing updates and his fourth edition was published in 2008. Since 2008 there have been major route changes to the GR11, especially in the Basque Country and Navarre. Road walking has been reduced to a minimum, the route has been well signed and waymarked and the GR11 has now developed into a magnificent route through largely unspoilt and wild mountains. This completely new guide includes all changes made in the route to 2013.

It is now just about possible to walk the GR11 without camping or using bothies and this new guide is organised into 45 stages for the benefit of those who are using accommodation along the route. Walkers who, like the author, prefer wild camping in the mountains will find much greater flexibility in their planning.

Brian Johnson

Lac Redon and Lac Long (Stage 24)

INTRODUCTION

Punta Chistau (Stage 19)

The Pyrenees is the mountain chain which forms the border between France and Spain, stretching over 400km from the Atlantic Ocean to the Mediterranean Sea. The GR11, which stays on the Spanish side of the border, provides a very varied scenic route through magnificent, often remote, high or deserted mountains.

As the GR11 leaves the border town of Irún on the Atlantic coast it follows ridges on the gentle grassy and wooded hills of the Basque Country and Navarre. There is then a rapid transition into steep limestone mountains, passing through the world-renowned Ordesa Canyon before the fantastic granite peaks of the High Pyrenees are reached. The High Pyrenees rise to over 3000m, with snowfields surviving well into the summer and the remnants of the glaciers which carved out the deep

valleys. The GR11 generally heads up these alpine valleys before crossing a high pass and descending into the next valley. These rough, tough mountains continue into Andorra. The mountains become gentler once Andorra is passed but, surprisingly, the highest point on the GR11 is reached after the High Pyrenees are left behind. As the Mediterranean is approached the GR11 follows a line of steep, rugged, wooded hills to reach the sea at the spectacular peninsula of Cap de Creus.

NATIONAL AND NATURAL PARKS

The GR11 passes through two National Parks and six Natural Parks:
* Parque Natural de Valles Occidentales
* Parque Nacional de Ordesa y Monte Perdido

- Parque Natural de Posets-Maladeta
- Parc Nacional d'Aigüestortes i Estany de Sant Maurici
- Parc Natural Alt Pirineu
- Parc Natural Valls de Comapedrosa
- Parc Natural Val del Madriu
- Parc Natural Cap de Creus

The Valles Occidentales (western valleys) of Aragón is predominantly composed of limestone and is a relatively gentle introduction to the tough alpine terrain ahead of you.

Ordesa and Monte Perdido, a UNESCO World Heritage site, is the largest limestone massif in Western Europe. The highest peak is Monte Perdido (3355m) but it is the deep valleys, with thundering cascades and waterfalls edged by towering limestone, which attract the tourist.

Posets-Maladeta is a granite massif containing half the 3000m summits in the Pyrenees including Aneto (3404m), the highest mountain in the Pyrenees. Highly glaciated granite mountains provide some of the most spectacular mountain scenery in the world with thousands of little sparkling lakes nestling in a landscape dominated by bare rock.

As you pass into Catalonia, you pass through Aigüestortes and Sant Maurici National Park, another magical granite massif, and then the Parc Natural Alt Pirineu, the largest Natural Park in Catalonia. Alt Pirineu continues into Andorra as the Parc Natural Valls de Comapedrosa. The Val del Madriu as you leave Andorra is the final alpine section, with more fine granite scenery.

The GR11 ends with the Parc Natural Cap de Creus, which is a complete contrast: a rocky dry region, with almost no trees, on a peninsula sticking out into the Mediterranean Sea.

FROM THE ATLANTIC TO THE MEDITERRANEAN

There are three long-distance paths along the Pyrenees from the Atlantic to the Mediterranean:
- GR10
- High-level route (Haute Randonnée Pyrénénne, HRP)
- GR11 (La Senda Pirenaica)

The oldest and most popular of these routes is the GR10, which is entirely in France. This well-waymarked path spends much of its time in the foothills climbing up and down steep forested ridges with only occasional visits above the treeline. Frequent visits to towns and villages means accommodation and supplies are not usually a problem, but wild camping is not so easy. Staying to the north of the watershed, the GR10 has a much cooler and cloudier climate than on the GR11.

The HRP, which passes through France, Spain and Andorra, is not so much a walk as a mountaineering expedition. The route is not waymarked, except where it coincides with other routes, and you must expect to get lost! There is a lot of very rough terrain, including some very steep, possibly dangerous descents, and a lot of snow can be expected until late summer. Visits to towns and villages are infrequent so resupply is difficult and you will have to camp most of the time. You will spend a lot of time on high mountain ridges with a serious risk of thunderstorms and even fresh snow. The HRP is a daunting route for the inexperienced but is a magnificent expedition for those with the right experience.

The GR11 is a well-waymarked path which passes through Spain and Andorra. Like the HRP, it crosses many high mountain passes where there are boulderfields, scree and some easy scrambling at about the maximum difficulty the inexperienced would want when carrying a heavy rucksack. The weather tends to be considerably sunnier and drier than on the GR10 and thunderstorms are less of a problem than on the HRP as you don't spend long periods on high ridges. Frequent visits to towns and villages mean that resupply isn't much of a problem. Those who prefer not to camp or bivouac will find that a few of the days are rather long and that some of the alternative routes featured in this guide will need to be taken.

There could be problems with snow in early season, but not later in the summer. Although the GR11 stays much higher than the GR10, there is actually considerably less climbing or ascent.

The author considers the GR11 to be a far superior, although tougher, walk than the GR10. Unless you are an experienced mountaineer you should prefer the GR10 or GR11 to the HRP.

THE GR11

The total route is about 820km long with 46,000m of ascent and is described here in 45 stages. It can be seen as breaking into three broad sections.

- The first 10 stages through the lower and more verdant Basque Country and Navarre, gradually climbing into the higher mountains south

Col d'Angliós from Ibón d'Angliós (Stage 21)

of Lescun before dropping to the Puerto de Somport cross-Pyrenees (Jaca–Pau) road. This section covers about 210km, and includes some long initial stages.

• The High Pyrenees section from Candanchú through to Puigcerdà to the E of Andorra is covered in 25 stages and 380km, taking in the most remote and beautiful parts of the mountains. Access to the route, if needed, can be through Torla, Benasque, Espot and Encamp before reaching the busy main road/rail access at Puigcerdà running between Barcelona and Toulouse.

• The final section runs through Catalonia from Puigcerdà to the Mediterranean, and is described in 10 stages, covering about 230km. It is here that the GR11 reaches its highest point (2780m) before crossing steep wooded terrain and descending to the dry and probably hot coast at Cap de Creus.

As well as these main access points, at many places the route crosses smaller mountain roads serving high villages, generally well-served by bus, allowing the trekker to access or leave the route. Most routes quickly reach main bus and rail routes including the east/west rail lines between Bilbao, Pamplona, Zaragoza, Lleida and Barcelona in Spain or Hendaye, Pau, Toulouse and Perpignan in France.

Walkers with earlier editions of the Cicerone guide to the GR11, or maps such as the Prames or IGN maps, should note that there was a considerable rerouting of the GR11 between 2008 and 2011 and the GR11 is no longer shown correctly on these maps.

The GR11 doesn't pass over many summits, but suggestions are made for climbing many of the easier peaks which could be attempted while walking the route. If you want to climb some of the more difficult, higher peaks you should ask for advice from the guardians of the refuges.

It would be possible to walk the GR11 from Mediterranean to Atlantic, but this guide describes the route from the Atlantic so that you have the prevailing wind/rain on your back and have time to acclimatise to the heat before reaching the Mediterranean.

WEATHER AND WHEN TO GO

The Spanish south-facing slopes of the Pyrenees are much sunnier and drier than the French side and although you can expect good weather, you should be prepared for rain and thunderstorms. The hills of the Basque Country and Navarre have a reputation for mist and spells of gentle rain, but the author has known temperatures approaching 40°C.

The weather in the Central Pyrenees is often hot and dry, but these are high mountains and can be subject to terrific thunderstorms. Thunderstorms in high mountains are usually thought of as being an afternoon phenomenon, but in the Pyrenees the storms are often slow to build up and can arrive in the evening or even in the middle of the night! As the Mediterranean is approached you are reaching an arid region and can expect hot sunny weather.

Summer snowfall is unusual, but the author has experienced snow as low as 1500m on the GR11 in August. In 2012 there was hardly any snow

Vignemale from Barranco deros Batans in July 2012 (top), and then in July 2013 (Stage 14)

Chisagüés on the descent to Parzán (Stage 17)

on the high passes when the author through-hiked the GR11 with a mid-June start, and there would have been no problem starting in early June. However, a mid-June start in 2013 was a serious mountaineering expedition and there was still significant snow on the high passes well into August. Snow conditions vary tremendously from year to year. The inexperienced would be advised to wait for late June or July before setting off from Irún.

The best months to walk the GR11 are July, August and September, but if you are only intending to walk the lower sections of the GR11 in the Basque Country, Navarre or Catalonia you may prefer May, June, or October when the weather will be cooler.

WILDLIFE

The Pyrenees are a very popular with birdwatchers. The mountains act as a big barrier to migrating birds and in the spring and autumn they funnel birds along the Atlantic and Mediterranean coastlines and through the lower passes. The casual birdwatcher will be most impressed with the large number of birds of prey.

The massive Griffon vulture, with a wingspan of about 2.5m, will frequently be seen soaring on the high ridges, while the smaller Egyptian vulture, which is distinctively coloured with a white body and black-and-white wings, is also likely to be seen. You may also see Europe's largest and rarest vulture, the lammergeier, which has a wingspan of up to 2.8m. The lammergeier feeds mainly on bone marrow which it gets at

*Clockwise from top L to centre: Edelweiss, Anemone narcissiflora,
Gentian, White Asphodel, Martagon Lily, Great Yellow Gentian,
Aquilegia vulgaris, Androsace villosa, Bracket fungus*

You are bound to see – or hear – a marmot!

by dropping bones from a great height to smash on the rocks below. Golden, booted, short-toed and Bonelli's eagles may be seen. Arguably, the most beautiful bird you will see is the red kite with its deeply forked tail. You can also expect to see black kites, buzzards and honey buzzards as well as smaller birds of prey such as the kestrel, peregrine falcon, sparrowhawk and rarer birds such as the goshawk and even a migrating osprey.

One species which seems to be thriving is the alpine chough, which you will see in large flocks. This member of the crow family is all black except for a yellow bill and red legs. Rarer small birds to look out for are the wallcreeper, crossbill, crested tit, red-backed shrike, bullfinch and alpine accentor.

You are much less likely to see some of the rare mammals which used to frequent the Pyrenees. There

are no Pyrenean brown bears left on the Spanish side of the border and the Pyrenean Ibex seems to be extinct. Fortunately, you will have frequent sightings of the chamois (*isard/izard*) which was hunted to near extinction for the production of chamois leather, but has now made a remarkable recovery with numbers increasing to about 25,000. Other mammals you will see include marmot, several species of deer, fox, red squirrel and the reintroduced mouflon. There are badgers and wild boar, although these are less likely to be seen.

The most notable of these are the marmots, which are large ground squirrels that live in burrows. You will certainly know they are present when you hear their alarm signal, a loud whistle which sends them scurrying back into their burrows.

You are likely to see many reptiles and amphibians including several species of snake, lizard, toad, frog and the dramatic fire salamander.

Pyrenean plant life is very diverse with at least 160 species of flower endemic to the Pyrenees, as well as many species, such as edelweiss, which will be familiar to those visiting the Alps.

GETTING TO THE START

Access to the GR11 will be by car, coach, train or plane. (Useful websites are given in Appendix D.)

By car

You could to drive down to Irún through France or from Bilbao or Santander (by ferry from Portsmouth or Plymouth with Brittany Ferries) in northern Spain. You will need to find somewhere to leave your car and at the end of your walk you could return to Irún by rail.

By coach

It is possible to reach the Pyrenees by overnight coach from London (Victoria Coach Station). National Express run links to London and then Eurolines run coaches throughout Europe. The most convenient destinations for those walking the GR11 are Irún and Figueras. Eurolines also operate services to Bayonne, Orthez, Pau, Tarbes, San-Gaudens, Toulouse and Perpignan in northern France.

By rail

Paris can be reached by Eurostar. From here SNCF run high-speed trains to a variety of destinations including Hendaye, Pau, Toulouse and Perpignan. Although the GR11 is in Spain you will probably find the rail links on the French side of the Pyrenees are more useful for those wanting to hike sections of the GR11. You can connect with the GR11 using SNCF services to Hendaye, Candanchú (Col du Somport), Latour-de-Carol or Cerbère.

Hendaye is the French border town adjacent to Irún. From Pau you can take a train to Oloron-Ste-Marie then SNCF bus to Candanchú. From Toulouse there are trains to Latour-de-Carol which is only an hour's walk from the GR11 at Puigcerdà. There are trains from Perpignan to Cerbère and then frequent trains crossing the border from Cerbère to Llançà, on the GR11. There is also a useful rail link from Perpignan to Villefranche and on by narrow-gauge railway (Train Jaune) to Latour-de-Carol

or a direct bus link from Perpignan to Latour-de-Carol.

The main west–east line joins Hendaye, Pau, Toulouse and Perpignan.

By plane

At the time of writing, Ryanair fly from Stansted and some regional airports in the UK to Biarritz, Lourdes, Carcassonne, Perpignan, Gerona and Barcelona. British Airways fly direct to Toulouse and Barcelona. Air France have flights from London to Pau and a big choice of destinations if you fly via Paris. Easyjet fly from London to Biarritz and Bristol or London to Toulouse.

GETTING HOME

There is no public transport from Cap de Creus. Your main option is to walk or hitch a lift to Cadaqués, which has now developed as a holiday resort.

From Cadaqués there are frequent buses to Figueras from where you can get trains to Cerbère to connect to the French rail network. There are also buses to Barcelona and Barcelona Airport. From Barcelona you could connect with the French rail network by taking a train to Puigcerdà (Latour-de-Carol).

If you have time to spare you could walk back to Port de la Selva, exploring some of the beaches on the Cap de Creus peninsular, and then follow part of the coastal path, the GR92, to Llançà or even to Cerbère.

EQUIPMENT

This is a serious expedition so you should have previous experience of backpacking or long-distance walks

GR11 hikers at Coll de Tudela (Stage 28)

before attempting this fantastic route. A few general points are made on equipment here.

- Keep your load as light as possible. If you don't need it, don't carry it!
- If you are using accommodation you may still want to carry a lightweight sleeping bag and camping mat to enable you to bivouac if necessary.
- Your waterproofs should be able to cope with thunderstorms in the High Pyrenees or steady rain in the Basque Country.
- You should have sufficient clothing to cope with sub-zero temperatures.
- A sun-hat is strongly recommended.
- Use plenty of sun-screen.
- Shorts are preferred by most hikers.
- Good quality walking boots are the best footwear. You could use lightweight boots, but heavy boots aren't

necessary. Trainers aren't really robust enough for the terrain. Make sure you have a good tread on your shoes or boots.

- As a minimum you should have containers capable of carrying 4 litres of water, possibly with one easily accessible water bottle and the remaining capacity as water bags.
- It is recommended that you use two walking poles to aid climbing, protect the knees on steep descents, to provide stability when crossing rough terrain, snowfields or mountain streams and for protection from dogs! If you are not carrying walking poles you may need an ice-axe to cope with snow on the high passes. Crampons may be needed in early season in a high snow year.

CULTURE AND LANGUAGE

Spanish holidays

The main Spanish holiday season is from about 15 July–20 August. During this period all facilities will be open, but accommodation could be fully booked, especially at weekends.

Spanish siesta

You can expect shops to be open in the morning, closed during the afternoon and open again in the evening. In larger towns they are more likely to be open all day.

Languages

Although you may think you are walking through the 'Spanish' Pyrenees, the locals won't think of themselves primarily as Spanish.

You are passing through Euskadi (Basque Country), Navarra (Navarre), Aragón, Andorra and Cataluña (Catalonia). In the Basque Country and the north of Navarre the main language is Euskera (Basque) and in Catalonia it is Catalán. It is less likely that you will encounter Aragonés and Aranés but you will see the legacy of these languages in

Catalan flag, Molló

the confusion of place names. Spanish (Castilian) will be an official language in these provinces and you can expect all the locals to speak Spanish as a second language. English is now spoken much more widely than it was in the 20th century, especially by younger people, and is gradually taking over from French as a third language.

There is a lot of confusion with place names in the Pyrenees, with many different spellings. When Spain was a centralised fascist state, Spanish names were imposed on the provinces, but with the coming of democracy, the provinces have been able to show a greater degree of independence and one expression of this is the return to place names in the local language. This means that on maps and signposts names may be given in Spanish, a local language, or even in French.

Politics

When they were independent states, the Basque Country and Catalonia were much larger than at present and included large chunks of the Pyrenees which are now in France. They have a great deal of autonomy and the independence movements in both provinces have a lot of support.

The Spanish Civil War had a devastating effect on the people of the Pyrenees and the effects can still be seen today with the destruction or desertion of many mountain villages. The Civil War broke out in 1936 with a coup d'état by reactionary elements in the army. The position in the Pyrenees was particularly complicated as there were not only the Fascist and Republican armies, but also independence movements among the

23

Catalans and the Basques. By the time the Republicans were defeated in 1939 about 700,000 lives had been lost and about 500,000 refugees had fled across the Pyrenees into France.

Andorra

Although Andorra is not in the European Union (EU), it uses the Euro. Be aware that if you buy 'duty free' products, you have not paid tax in an EU country and customs controls are in operation on road crossings to France or Spain. Catalán is the official language of Andorra, but English, French and Spanish are widely spoken. Camping laws are the same as in Spain: no daytime camping, except with the landowner's permission, but you can bivouac (with or without a tent) on uncultivated land away from habitation. Fires are not permitted!

ACCOMMODATION

There is a wide range of accommodation on the GR11.

- *Paradors* are luxurious and expensive hotels.
- Hotels vary greatly in quality and cost but they would have all the facilities you expect of an hotel in Britain.
- *Hostals* are basic hotels. Some will just offer accommodation, but most will also have a bar-restaurant (a *hostal* is not a hostel).
- *Pensions* are rather like the British guest house.
- *Casa Rural* or *Turisme Rural* are private houses offering accommodation similar to the British bed & breakfast.

Refugio de Biadós (Stages 18 and 19)

Pico Llena Cantal over Refugio de Respomuso (Stage 12)

- *Albergue* are 'youth hostels', but as in Britain they do take adults.
- Manned *Refugios* or *Refugi* are mountain huts which offer accommodation (possibly in communal dormitories). They have a drink and meals service, open to both residents and non-residents and will often provide packed lunches.
- Many campgrounds will have cabins, normally called 'bungalows', and some will have bunkhouse accommodation.
- Unmanned *Refugios* or *Refugi* are open for the use of mountaineers and walkers. They are equivalent to the Scottish 'bothy'. They range in quality from purpose-built buildings which are well maintained by mountaineering clubs to buildings which are no better than unmaintained cow sheds.

The facilities described during the course of each stage description are summarised in a box at the end of each stage, in route order, with full contact details.

If desperate ask at the bar-restaurant; they will often know locals who are willing to offer accommodation outside the official system.

Manned mountain refuges

Refuges vary greatly, but as a guideline you can expect the following:
- Basic accommodation for walkers and climbers.
- Refuge hours and rules are designed for walkers, not for late-night drinkers.
- You may be able to get a discount if you are a member of an Alpine Association.
- People staying in refuges usually book half board (supper, bed and breakfast) or full board (half board

GR11 hiker above Estany de Monges (Stage 23)

with the addition of a picnic bag for lunch).

- Some, but not all refuges, will have self-catering facilities.
- There are mattresses and blankets in the dormitories but you need to bring a sleeping bag or a sheet bag.
- Some refuges are open all year and others only during the summer. Many will only be open at weekends in the spring or autumn and some will open out of season if you make a reservation.
- It is recommended that you make reservations in high summer and at weekends.
- Refuges offer a bar and snack service to walkers outside of normal mealtimes.

- Refuges will normally have a room which can be used as a bothy when the refuge is closed.
- Camping is not permitted in the vicinity of most manned refuges.
- Many of the refuges don't have their own website, but use a regional website which operates central booking (see Appendix D).

CAMPING

In this guide the American term *campground* has been used for commercial or organised campsites, to distinguish them for wilderness campsites.

Car-camping used to be widespread alongside roads and dirt roads with visitors setting up camps, often for weeks at a time, in many of the most beautiful places in the mountains or around the coast. To prevent this, a law was passed to ban wild camping and this law is enforced by the police. As is often the case laws have unintended consequences and this law, intended to prevent car-camping and the setting up of long-term camps, also applied to backpackers.

The compromise, in practice, is that backpackers are allowed to bivouac for one night, with or without a small tent, well away from roads and habitation. This exception to the law has been defined in some areas such as in the Ordesa National Park, where camping is allowed between sunrise and sunset above 2100m, and in 'Parc Natural' in Catalonia, where wild camping is permitted between 8pm and 8am.

You should ask permission if you want to camp near villages, in farmers' fields, or close to a refuge. There is rarely any problem camping high in the mountains but discretion should be used when camping at lower levels. The daily stages given in this guide are intended for those using overnight accommodation. Those who are wild camping will want to ignore these stages and camp well away from the towns, villages and refuges.

If you are accustomed to always camping beside water you will often have difficulty in finding a suitable campsite, especially in the Basque Country and eastern Catalonia. In the High Pyrenees camping beside streams often means you are sharing the grass with cows and mosquitoes. If you are prepared to camp away from water, you have much more flexibility and you can often find campsites with spectacular views.

Suggestions have been made in this guide as to the best campsites. These will normally be places where camping overnight is legal and with good grass

West summit, Tuca d'Angliós, from Estany Cap de Llauset (Stage 21)

which will take a tent peg. The experienced backpacker will find plenty of other places to camp.

The author tends to camp as high as possible. Not only is there magnificent scenery, it's legal and there is less chance of being disturbed. What is more, there are likely to be fewer cows, better grass, and fewer mosquitos and biting insects.

The three types of camping gas commonly available are:

- The ones you pierce, referred to in this guide as 'original' cylinders.
- 'Easy-clic' resealable cylinders, the main resealable system used in Southern Europe.
- Screw-on resealable cylinders, such as manufactured by Coleman and Primus; these are the most widely used in Britain, northern Europe and USA and in this guide have been called 'Coleman-style' gas cylinders.

Where these are mentioned in the text they were in stock when the author passed through in 2013, but it cannot be guaranteed that they will be in stock when you pass through. 'Coleman-style' cylinders are becoming more readily available, but the locals mainly use the 'original' or 'easy-clic' cylinders and these still have greater availability. Liquid fuels are most likely to be available at the *ferreteria* (ironmongers) but make sure you know what you are buying!

WATER

Water can be a problem if the weather is hot. When walking in temperatures of 25–30°C, you will need at least ½ litre (1 pint) of water for each hour of walking, plus about 2 litres for a 'dry' camp, (ie one without a source of water). This is a guideline; actual needs will vary considerably from person to person and will depend on the temperature.

Most towns, villages and hamlets in the Pyrenees have fountains with untreated spring water. The locals and most walkers will drink the water without further treatment.

You will often find fountains or 'piped' water as you walk along the trail. It should be obvious whether this water comes from a spring or a surface stream. Spring water is usually of a high quality and can be drunk with confidence. You should be more cautious about surface streams, especially woodland streams or streams in areas which are well stocked with sheep or cattle.

Unless otherwise indicated the streams, springs and water-points mentioned in the text were running both in

Swedish GR11 hiker collecting water from a stream (Stage 2)

GR11 waymarks

2012, a dry year, and in 2013, a wet year, on through-hikes starting from Irún in mid-June. During snow melt and in a wet year there will be far more water sources, especially in the High Pyrenees.

USING THIS GUIDE

The route has been split into stages with the walker who wants to use accommodation in mind. Those who are camping are advised to ignore these sections and

to camp well away from towns and villages. Accommodation is limited at the endpoint of some sections so booking would be advisable in peak season. There are some sections where those requiring accommodation will have to follow the alternative route given rather than the 'main' route.

In good visibility, when the ground is free of snow, it is possible to follow the GR11 using the waymarking, route description and 1:100,000 maps in this guidebook, but we would always

Fresh snow on Pico Royo in August (Stage 19)

recommend carrying a map. You should certainly carry more detailed maps if you intend following the route in early season, when there could be extensive snowfields, or if you intend to cross high passes in bad weather.

Most navigational mistakes occur because the walker does not look at the map or guidebook until they are lost! The route descriptions and maps in the guide are designed to prevent you getting lost and they will be of little use when you are already lost! Keep the guidebook handy, not buried in your rucksack.

Note on the maps

The base maps used in this guide were developed from publicly available information. The contours are generally very good, and other tracks and paths are taken from open source information and they are considered to give a reasonable representation of the area and features surrounding the route.

Water information has only been checked on the route of the GR11; streams shown on the route can be expected to run throughout the summer and the water-points marked on the map are likely to be reliable through the summer.

Not all **tracks and paths** are marked. This is particularly noticeable at the Atlantic and Mediterranean ends of the route where mapping the multitude of paths and tracks would have made the maps unreadable.

Timings

The timings given in this guide are the actual walking times recorded by the author when he backpacked the route in 2012 and 2013. This does not include time for breaks or breathers and actual walking time will depend on other factors such as navigational ability, fitness, load and conditions. Times to climb peaks assume you are walking without a pack.

Distances, climb and height profiles

Distances don't mean very much in the Pyrenees, where the steepness or roughness of the terrain can be a lot more important than the distance or the amount of climb. Distances and climb have been estimated from the maps. The height profiles are intended to show the general trend of the day's walk and won't show all ups and downs.

GPS

A GPS device is not needed to follow the GR11, but GPS co-ordinates (latitude and longitude) have been included for key points along the route for those who insist on using one. At the time of writing the 'free' maps of the GR11 that you can download from the internet for use with GPS are too inaccurate to be worth bothering with.

THE GR11

Dolmen de Achar Aguas Tuertas (Stage 10)

GETTING TO CABO DE HIGUER
FROM IRÚN

The simplest solution is to take a taxi from Irún to Cabo de Higuer. In summer there are buses (route E25) about every 15min from Paseo Colón, in the centre of Irún, to Playa de Hondarribia. It would take about 1hr 50min to walk to Cabo de Higuer from Irún or 2hr 15min from Hendaye Railway Station in France.

You need to continue past the Playa de Hondarribia, the main beach of Hondarribia, to reach the harbour at the N end of the sea-front. Follow the road which climbs steeply from the N end of the harbour switchbacking up to a junction. Turn right to reach the S side of the lighthouse, Faro de Cabo Higuer, and Camping Faro de Higuer (40m, N43°23.479 W001°47.546).

Faro de Cabo Higuer

Camping Faro de Higuer has a bar-restaurant. Open all year. Tel 943 641 008 **www.campingseuskadi. com/faro**. See Stage 1 for facilities in Hondarribia and Irún.

STAGE 1
Cabo de Higuer to Bera (Vera de Bidosoa)

Start	Cabo de Higuer
Distance	30km
Total Ascent/Descent	1100m
Difficulty	Easy. Waymarking does not begin until the S edge of Irún, after which it is very good.
Time	8hr 5min
High Points	Collado de Erlaitz (448m), Collado de Tellería (415m)

Stage 1 is too long for a first day unless you are already 'trail fit'. If you are camping it is sensible to take three days to get to Elizondo at the end of Stage 2. If you are staying in Irún you could walk the section from Cabo de Higuer to Irún on the evening of your arrival and then set out from Irún in the morning. Once clear of Irún, the route is typical of the Basque Country as you traverse steep rolling hills on good tracks through a mixture of woodland and pasture.

There doesn't seem to be an official starting point for the GR11 but the **Faro de Higuer lighthouse** is the prominent feature on the cape. You could of course climb down the rocks to dip your toes in the Atlantic Ocean.

Follow the tarmac track, signed 'GR121 to Hondarribia', down between the lighthouse and the campground, soon forking left along a path which loops round the lighthouse and follows the slumping undercliff. On reaching the road, turn left down to the harbour and follow the coast road past the sandy **Playa de Hondarribia** (25min) where there are water-points, toilets and beach showers. There are water points at regular intervals along the seafront. Continue past the large marina and along the shore until the road turns inland alongside a canal opposite the airport (1hr).

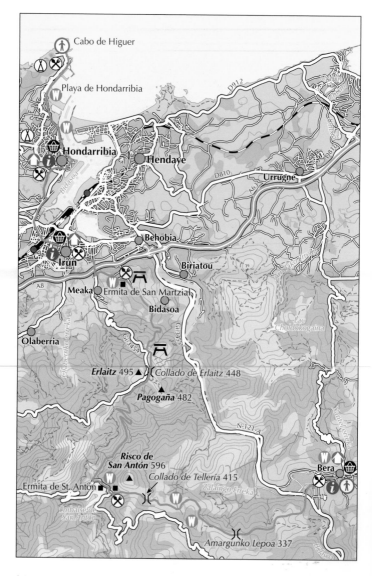

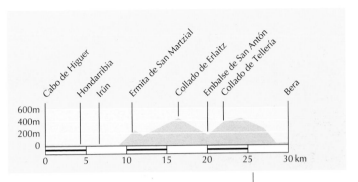

Hondarribia is a large tourist resort with all facilities. Camping Jaizkibel, 500m W of the centre of Hondarribia, also has cabins and bar-restaurant. Albergue Juan Sebastián Elcano is at the N end of Hondarribia, inland from the marina. You must show the youth hostelling international card in this youth hostel.

After the road veers right, go straight (W) across a double roundabout, fork left at the next small roundabout, past the Eroski supermarket, left at a big roundabout and immediately right down the Santa Engrazia Kalea. This road returns to the main road by the Puente de Amute (1hr 30min). After crossing the bridge, fork left along road GI-636 before veering left into **Irún**, under a road bridge, straight across a large roundabout and up the Calle de Fuenterribía. Fork left up Hondarribia Kalea and over the railway into the wide boulevard of the Paseo de Colón to reach a big square (1hr 50min).

Irún is a large town with an international railway station. All types of camping gas are available at Decathlon in Parque Comercial Txingudi which is in Ventas at the SW end of Irún near junction 2 of the A-8 autopista. There are buses to Txingudi from Hondarribia and Irún every hour.

Keep straight on as the road becomes the Avenida de Navarra after a large multi-way junction and heads downhill. Head down the right-hand side of this dual carriageway

Aldabe Farm, above Irún

and cross a stream. Turn right along the second road after the stream, turning left and immediately right at the end. Cross a roundabout and then, at the next roundabout, go diagonally left, signed to San Martzial Ermita. Cross a stream and turn right (S) along the Ibarrola road and under the **A-8** (Autopista del Cantábrico), after which there is a GR11 information board by a concrete track on your left (2hr 15min, 20m, N43°20.009 W001°46.634). The GR11 is well waymarked from here.

Turn left up the concrete track, forking left up a rough track when the concrete track veers off to the waterworks. Join another concrete track at Aldabe Farm, cross a road and continue up a tarmac track which becomes gravel after another house. Cross the road again and reach a large picnic area with water and toilets (2hr 40min, 205m, N43°19.869 W001°45.920). The building on your right is the **Ermita San Martzial**, which has a bar-restaurant.

Irún, on the border of the kingdoms of Navarre, Castile and France, belonged to Navarre, but became part of Castile in 1200. In 1522 Navarre raised an army, assisted by German and French mercenaries, to recapture Irún and they defeated a

Castilian army at the battle of Monte San Martzial on 30 June 1522. Success was honoured by the building of a chapel on the shoulder of the hill.

In 1813 Wellington was besieging the French garrison at San Sebastián when he had news of a relief force under General Soult. Wellington broke off the siege and marched his British and Spanish army to meet the French. On 31 August 1813 the Napoleonic troops were defeated in the second battle on Monte San Martzial and the chapel became an important shrine for the people of Irún.

Continue ESE along a concrete track, turning right 50m after a children's play area/picnic area. Don't get confused by the R-11 sign – this is a local footpath and nothing to do with the GR11. Keep straight on when the concrete track goes right and follow a track along the crest of the ridge, descending to a farm on a saddle. Keep straight on, ignoring a track to the right, and climb. You pass a small water catchment dam but the water is of dubious quality. Fork right after a cattle grid along a track which becomes concrete after passing a farm. Turn left up a rough track, under power lines, at the top of the hill. This track soon becomes a grassy path to reach a white cabin. Veer to the right of the cabin to reach a waterless picnic site beside the GI-3454 road. Continue just left of the road to a car park on the **Collado de Erlaitz** (4hr 5min, 448m, N43°18.314 W001°45.380) with Erlaitz (495m) on the right and Pogogaña (482m) on the left. Dry camping. ▶

It would be very easy to walk up Pagogaña from here.

Follow a grassy track parallel to and just left of the road, passing through another waterless picnic site. Continue until you reach a track going off diagonally left (438m) just after large parking areas on either side of the road. The GR11 forks left (S) down the track. Gradually descend, forking left and veering sharp right at a junction. ▶ The good track switchbacks down, reaching a clear-looking woodland stream at the final switchback. Continue down the track until you cross a cattle grid and come out at a small road. Turn right, uphill, to reach the W end of the **Embalse de San Antón** (Endara) dam (5hr 30min, 240m, N43°16.624 W001°46.494). Turn left across the dam and continue along the road to pass the **Ermita de St. Antón**, on your right (5hr 40min). This chapel has a water-point and a covered seating area.

The rocky peak ahead is Risco de San Antón (596m).

Turn left up a concrete track signed to the Bar-restaurante Ola-Berri, just after the chapel. Before you reach the bar, the GR11 turns right over a stile and up a path across pasture, then forks left as you enter the wood and climbs steeply to reach a concrete track at the **Collado de Tellería** (Collado de San Antón) (6hr 5min, 415m, N43°16.446 W001°45.513). You may prefer to stay on the concrete track left of the Bar-restaurante Ola-Berri, then switchback right and follow the track to the Collado de Tellería. Dry camping.

Continue E along the concrete track, descending past a farm and climbing again. Keep straight on at crossroads and fork right at some houses. Fork right up a track then left along the main track and left again. Turn left and right at a woodland stream and then join a concrete track at a farm with a water-point in the farmyard. Fork right and then left along a path which joins a track. Soon fork right as the track becomes a path and pass a small spring. Cross a concrete track at Alasta (357m) and follow the track along the crest of the ridge. Dry camping. Fork left after a white building at **Amargunko Lepoa** and contour to the next saddle, Amargaga Lepoa (7hr 10min, 304m). Take the middle track, then fork left, then right, then left again to start the descent to Bera. Follow the main track down to reach a minor road on the outskirts of **Bera**. Keep straight on at a crossroads before veering right to an old narrow bridge across the **Rio Bidasoa**.

There is a memorial plaque on the bridge to the men of the **Rifle Brigade** who died on 1 September 1813 defending the bridge against the French. During their retreat following defeat at the Battle of San Martzial, the French army reached San Miguel Bridge over the Rio Bidasoa at Bera. The river was in flood following a severe thunderstorm and the bridge was the only crossing point. The bridge was defended by a 70-man company of green-jacketed riflemen (well known to readers of the Sharpe novels by Bernard Cornwell or viewers of the TV films starring Sean Bean) under Captain Daniel Cadoux. This small company held the bridge against about 10,000 French troops for about 18 hours. Unfortunately, they were let down by Major General Skerret who refused to send help, despite being camped only a mile away with his Light

Memorial plaque on bridge at Bera

Brigade. When the rifle brigade eventually retreated they suffered heavy casualties and the French were allowed to escape from the trap.

Cross the bridge and follow the road into town, turning left along the main road to the town centre. Turn right at the Bar-restaurante Euskalduna and continue to the square, now a big car park, just after the tourist office (8hr 5min, 40m, N43°16.844 W001°40.928).

Bera is a small town with a tourist office (public toilets inside), a selection of accommodation and an excellent supermarket. Ferreteria Monola stocks 'original' and 'easy-clic' camping gas. Hostal Euskalduna is now just a bar-restaurant and no longer offers accommodation.

Facilities on Stage 1 (in route order)
Camping Jaizkibel: tel 943 641 679 www.campingjaizkibel.com
Albergue Juan Sebastián Elcano: tel 943 415 164 (Bookings tel: 901 100 090)
    www.gipuzkoa.net/albergues
Irún Tourist Office: tel 943 020 732 www.irun.org/turismo
Bera Tourist Office: tel 948 631 222
Hostal Auzoa: tel 948 631 584
Hostal Zalain: tel 948 631 106
Hotel Churrut: tel 948 625 540 www.hotelchurrut.com

STAGE 2
Bera to Elizondo

Start	Bera
Distance	31km
Total Ascent	1400m
Total Descent	1200m
Difficulty	Easy. Waymarking is good.
Time	7hr 40min
High Point	Santa Bárbara (396m), Collado Achuela (795m)

Today's walking is primarily on tracks through woodland and pasture, over steep rolling hills. This is a long day so early in a hike, but there is no obvious way to shorten it for those who are not camping.

map continues
on page 42

Head S from the GR11 information board along the right-hand side of the square and up a concrete track which passes to the right of a tennis court and public swimming pool before joining a tarmac road. Continue to a junction on a bend where there is a water-point. Fork right up a track, then left and left again past a house and onto a concrete track, before forking right up a track. Rejoin the track and follow it to the final house. Take the left-hand track, still climbing, then go sharp left at a track junction onto open hillside.

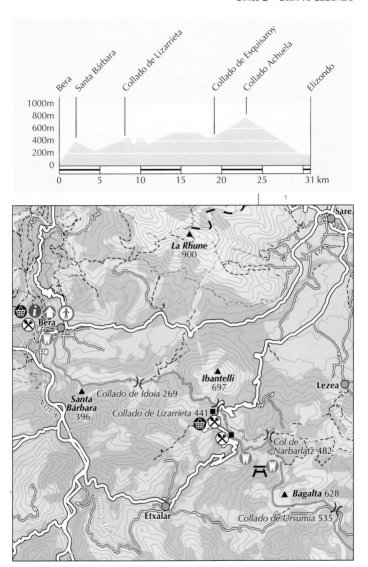

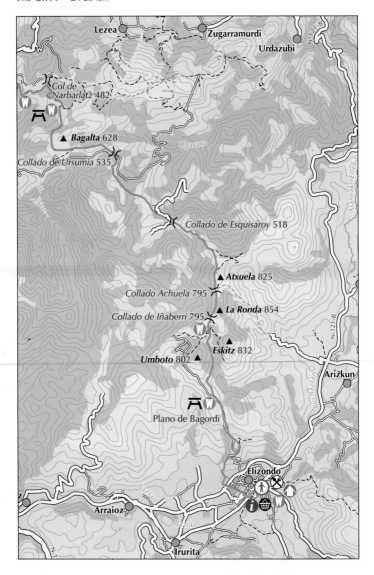

Fork right up the ridge to the summit of **Santa Bárbara** (1hr, 396m, N43°15.955 W001°40.310). On the summit you will find a concrete bunker and a collection of monuments and memorials.

> In 1939 Franco ordered the Pyrenean border to be **fortified and militarised**. The plan was to build more than 10,000 bunkers from one end of the Pyrenees to another. Initially, the reason for the fortifications was to prevent the return of the Republicans, but plans were modified to thwart a possible German invasion and finally to prevent intervention by the Allies or the Maquis (French resistance movement). Construction continued until 1952, long after there was any justification for the defences. You will see the remains of this defence line at intervals along the GR11.

Veer left along the edge of the wood, descending to a saddle and straight on up the other side. At the end of the wood descend through fields, picking up a concrete track to the right of a white house to reach the **Collado de Idoia** (1hr 25min, 269m).

The high mountain to the N is La Rhune (900m) in France. Turn diagonally right along a dirt road, forking left uphill. Higher up, fork right along a track, turn left at a junction by a barn, Dornakuko Borda, and fork right when you return to the dirt road by another barn. The road veers right as you reach the woods. Contour along the SW slopes of **Ibantelli** (697m) and cross a woodland stream. ▸ Continue to the Venta de Lizaieta at **Collado de Lizarrieta** (2hr 20min, 441m, N43°15.661 W001°37.157). This bar-restaurant has a small shop attached with a poor selection of overpriced food.

It would be wise to treat the water before drinking.

Cross the road and continue up a large track. After about 10min, at a saddle, a track joins from back right. The GR11 takes the path forking right and switchbacks down past Usategi bar-restaurant before forking left and climbing past a barn with water-point. Fork left to cross a ridge and then descend a little on the other side. The path then contours and passes another barn before reaching a junction just below the **Col de Narbarlatz** (3hr 5min, 445m, N43°15.170 W001°36.027). Fork right and continue downhill on bigger

Urrizpil and Umboto from W slope of La Ronda

paths. You soon pass water flowing from a pipe on the right, just below the trail, and descend to a woodland stream. Cross and veer right. Pass below the Casería Gorra Farm, turning left up a concrete track through the farmyard (3hr 15min, 370m). The water-point in the farmyard seems to be well protected by loose dogs! Continue up the track, turning sharp right at a junction with a dirt road and veering left to a picnic area with a water-point (3hr 30min, 440m). Discrete camping should be possible here.

Fork left at the picnic area and soon pass a pipe with flowing water. The track veers right, after which you ignore right turns and continue straight to the top of the hill, then stay on the main track past a barn and veer left round **Bagalta** (628m). Then fork left on a grassy path to rejoin the main track. Pass a barn at the Collado de Irazako (530m) then reach a power-line where there is an ancient tumulus. Stay on the main track, ignoring turns, to reach a complex road junction at the **Collado de Ursumia** (535m). Turn right (S) along a track, following the main track at a junction, then fork right at a col to start the descent. Fork left three times during the descent, then right along a path which contours through woods before joining a track just before reaching the road at **Collado de Esquisaroy** (5hr 50min, 518m, N43°13.010 W001°33.080). ▶

There is a sign down the road on the right to Casa Rural Landa Etxea, but the author has no information on this possible accommodation.

Cross the road and take the path forking right. Fork right at a junction (5hr 35min, 725m) with a small iron cross and fork right and left as you continue to climb to a track joining from the left. Traverse right (W) of Atxuela (825m) to **Collado Achuela** (5hr 55min, 795m) with another iron cross. The track contours W of La Ronda (854m) to reach the **Collado de Iñaberri** (6hr 5min, 795m, N43°11.522 W001°32.141). Excellent dry campsites.

Fork left, roughly S, ignoring a myriad of paths, then veer left into the woods and turn left down a good track and immediately right along a path which leads to Caserío de Maistruzar (6hr 15min). Immediately after the farmhouse is a spring, Fuente de Maistruzar. The path joins a track, and then forks right to reach a road at **Plano de Bagordi** (6hr 40min, 580m) where there is a picnic area with a water-point. Turn left along the road and after about 1km fork left down a path, the first of several 'shortcuts' (though it may be as easy to follow the road). Turn left on regaining the road. The next shortcut, also on the left, passes below a clay-pigeon shooting range. There is a sign advising you to stay on the road if you hear shooting. Go straight across when you next meet the road, then right along the road before taking a path to the left. Follow the path across the road when you next meet it (360m). You need to take this path as it does not return to this road, but brings you down to another minor road. Turn left and follow the road down to the Elizondo bypass, which will not be shown on older maps. Cross carefully and keep straight on into **Elizondo**, turning left along the main street to a large church on the right (7hr 40min, 200m). There is a water-point in the churchyard.

Elizondo is a small town with a seasonal tourist office and a range of accommodation. As well as smaller shops there is a large supermarket just NE of the church. Ferreteria Quevedo has 'original', 'easy-clic' and 'Coleman-style' camping gas.

Detail on the church at Elizondo

Facilities on Stage 2
Elizondo Tourist Office: tel 948 581 517
Hotel Saskaitz: tel 948 580 488
Hotel Baztan: tel 948 580 050 www.hotelbaztan.com
Hostal Antxitonea: tel 948 581 807 www.antxitonea.com
Eskisaroi Pension: tel 948 580 013
Albergue Kortarixar: tel 948 581 820 www.kortarixar.es
English speaking Mark Woldin offers bed and breakfast at his home as well as
    rides from the trail. Tel 660 976 422 markwoldin@gmail.com

STAGE 3

Elizondo to Puerto de Urkiago

Start	Elizondo
Distance	19km
Total Ascent	1100m
Total Descent	400m
Difficulty	Easy. The waymarking is good but you will have to take care with navigation in mist as the route is complex and undefined in places. It will be muddy and slippery in wet conditions.
Time	5hr 30min (7hr 40min to Albergue Sorogain in Stage 4)
High Point	Collado Bustalmorro (1170m)

The traditional end of Stage 3 is at the Puerto de Urkiaga, but this road pass is without accommodation, good campsites or water! The main option for those requiring accommodation would be to continue to Albergue Sorogain which is just over 2 hours ahead (see Stage 4). An alternative would be to use Hostal Arrobi Borda whose owners offer transport to and from the Puerto de Urkiaga.

The walking is primarily through woodland and pasture on paths and tracks over steep rolling hills. The route reaches 1000m for the first time. There are no obviously good campsites until you reach the Collado de Urballo.

Head up Avenida Monsenor Berecochea, immediately right (W) of the church. A left and right turn lead you out of town to reach a GR11 information board (216m, N43°08.542 W001°30.848). Fork right up a track, soon forking right and left before rejoining the road. Follow the road for about 100m then turn right along a grass track which veers left into a path. Turn left at a track and immediately right. Turn right when the track continues through a gate, then fork left up a path, passing right of a farm. Join a track and turn right along a path (45min, 361m) as you come close to the road.

Continue climbing, cross a concrete track (1hr) and pass a spring (435m). When the track switchbacks right, veer left along a path and pass a better spring. Higher up cross a

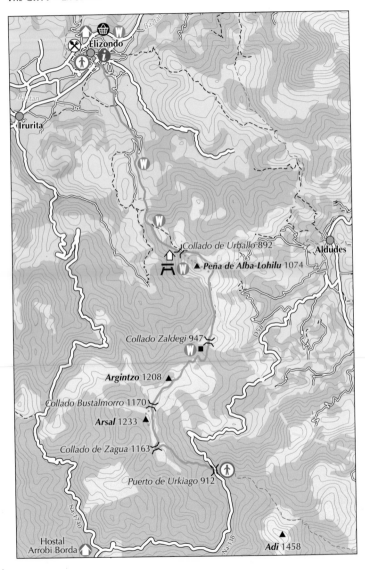

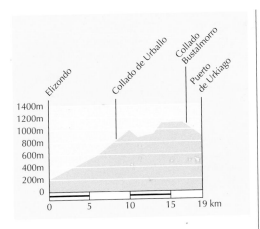

stream and keep straight on, steadily climbing until you reach a track (1hr 40min, 470m, N43°06.373 W001°29.730). Turn right, then fork left at a switchback on a major track. Keep straight on along a grass track when the major track bends left, soon passing a water-point (20m left of the track). The track narrows to a path and climbs gradually to arrive at a hunter's cabin (2hr 30min, 888m, N43°05.664 W001°29.000) just below the **Collado de Urballo**. The hunters' cabin has water-point, picnic tables and a 2-man bothy. Continue up to the col. Camping is possible at the col. ▶

In good visibility you could easily climb Peña de Alba-Lohilu (1074m) to the SE.

Hunter's cabin at Collado de Urballo

Keep straight on up the earthen track, soon forking right up a path. The paths are a bit nebulous with many sheep tracks, so follow the waymarks carefully as you contour the grassy N flank of Peña de Alba-Lohilu and reach the border fence at Border Stone 127.

In 1659 the **Treaty of the Pyrenees** was signed on an island in the Rio Bidasoa to end the 1635–1659 war between France and Spain, and a new border was fixed at the Pyrenees. However, the border was not properly settled until the Treaty of Limits in 1856. Border Stone 127 is one of about 600 numbered stones that were positioned in the 1860s to designate the border.

Pass ancient tumuli as you follow the fence along the ridge. Eventually, after a couple of shooting towers, leave the border fence as it veers off left. Soon reach another fence, which also veers off left before you reach an earthen track. Fork right at a gate to reach a hunting cabin with a waterpoint and benches at **Collado Zaldegi** (3hr 45min, 947m, N43°03.932 W001°28.536). The water-point was not working in 2013, but a nearby stream was running. Camping is possible here, with better dry campsites on the ridge ahead.

Veer right up the track, and right again to the right of two more hunters' cabins to pick up a path heading NW, before swinging SW. Pay careful attention to the waymarks in this area as there are many sheep tracks, which are often more significant than the GR11. Climb out of the woods and steeply up to a col below Argintzo (1208m). Cross the fence at a stile (4hr 15min, 1139m, N43°03.613 W001°29.089) and veer right, to the left of the fence. Follow waymarks along faint animal tracks round the SE flank of Argintzo to rejoin the ridge and fence, at a saddle (4hr 30min, 1158m).

The route contours a few metres below **Collado Bustalmorro** (1170m) with signpost. ◄ There is a little confusion here as there are old waymarks close to the ridge and newer waymarks further down the slope. They both lead to the broad grassy **Collado de Zagua** (5hr, 1163m, N43°02.464 W001°29.596).

It would be easy to climb Arsal (1233m) on your right rather than contour its E slopes.

The GR12 continues along the ridge, but turn left on the GR11, veering right of a white cabin. Take care to follow the waymarks to locate the path through the woods. Pass a

cabin where you pick up a track which is followed, ignoring all side-turns, to the N-138 road at **Puerto de Urkiago** (5hr 30min, 912m, N43°02.158 W001°28.209).

Sheep shearing below Collado de Zagua

This minor road connects Aldudes in France to Zubiri in Spain. There is little traffic on this cross-border road so it could be difficult to hitch the 20km down (S) to Zubiri, on the Camino de Santiago, where there is accommodation. While it would be possible to camp here, there aren't any good sites. In an emergency you could use one of the old wartime concrete bunkers on the route ahead.

Hostal Arrobi Borda, which is just up the NA-1740, about 6km down the NA-138, has accommodation and bar-restaurant, and offers free lifts to and from the GR11 from the Puerto de Urkiago for those staying at the hostal.

Facilities on Stage 3
Hostal Arrobi Borda: tel 948 304 709 www.arrobiborda.com
Hosteria de Zubiri: tel 948 304 329 www.hosteriadezubiri.com

STAGE 4

Puerto de Urkiaga to Burguete (Auritz)

Start	Puerto de Urkiaga
Distance	18km
Total Ascent/Descent	800m
Difficulty	Easy. You are following small paths for much of the section and will need to keep a close eye on the waymarking.
Time	4hr 55min
High Point	Collado Aratun (1212m), Menditixipi (1213m)

The route crosses two grassy ridges before descending a wooded river valley. If you have any excess energy a visit Roncesvalles would be worthwhile. You are getting into country where you can expect to see Griffon vulture and red kite.

Head up the concrete track, passing a locked hut, and soon turn left up a waymarked route through the woods which shortcuts back to the track. Continue up the concrete track which becomes a dirt track as the gradient eases. Fork left (35min) and then fork right as the track splits into

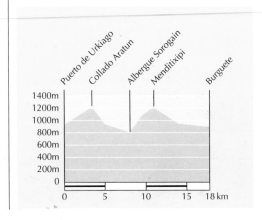

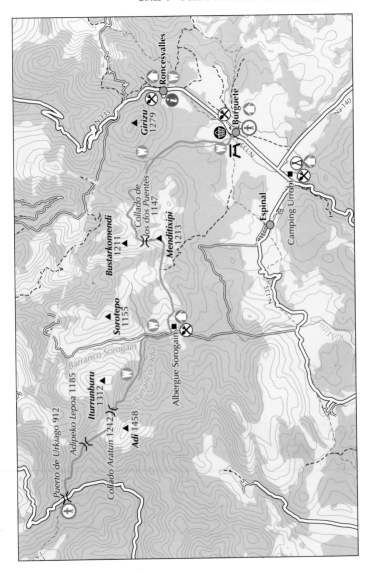

two poor tracks. At about 1175m fork left along a path to reach a gate at **Adipeko Lepoa** (50min, 1185m, N43°01.611 W001°26.812). Good dry campsites. Turn right along small paths which start just above the wood opposite. Contour on grassland along the N slopes of Adi (1458m), passing a small seasonal spring, before picking up a track through the woods to reach a grassy saddle, **Collado Aratun** (1hr 5min, 1212m, N43°01.383 W001°26.230). Good dry campsites.

Veer right to a stile over a fence and drop down steeply. Take care not to lose the waymarked route and eventually reach the confluence of two clear-looking woodland streams (at about 940m). Continue left of the **Barranco Odia**, crossing it on a metal bridge (895m) and crossing it again (865m), possibly getting wet feet. There are now good campsites as you follow the stream down to the minor road in the Sorogain valley. You may prefer to follow the road S from here, but the waymarked route veers right, recrosses the **Barranco Sorogain** and follows its right-hand bank. Cross the stream, possibly now dried up, as you approach the **Albergue Sorogain** (2hr 10min, 840m, N43°00.390 W001°24.555).

Albergue Sorogain offers accommodation and has a bar-restaurant.

Head roughly E from just N of the Albergue Sorogain and climb past a small wind turbine. Keep a close eye on the waymarks as you are following nebulous sheep tracks which head up the grassy hill. Eventually reach a fence which is followed to a track (1069m). Continue up grassland, beside the fence to the top of the hill (3hr 15min, 1181m). Cross the fence and follow it E to a saddle (1141m) and up the other side, turning left along a fence at the top to the summit of **Menditixipi** (3hr 30min, 1213m, N43°00.611 W001°22.495).

Continue N, crossing a fence to pick up a track just before the **Collado de los dos Puentes** (1147m). Veer right along the track to Uztarketako Lepoa (1116m). Continue along the grassy track to a minor top, Atalozti (3hr 50min, 1113m, N43°01.160 W001°21.917). The GR12 goes straight on from here but the GR11 turns right (ESE) down a grassy ridge, passing a sculpture, to enter the woods. Descend on a track through the woods and cross a woodland stream which you follow downstream. There are good campsites alongside the stream. Continue to a gate where you join a tarmac track (4hr

GR11 hikers on Menditixipi

45min, 898m). This is followed to **Burguete** which is reached by the church (4hr 55min, 898m, N42°59.348 W001°20.154).

Burguete is a village with good facilities for tourists to cater for Camino de Santiago walkers. Turn left up the road for Hostal Burguete and, at the top of the village, a well-stocked supermarket beside a picnic area with water and toilets. Turn right down the road for Hostal Juandeaburre and Hotel Loizu, which offers discounts to hikers. There are also several Casa Rural offering accommodation in the village. Camping Urrobi, which is about 2km SW of Burguete, has a 42-bed hostel and cabins as well as camping facilities and a small shop with 'original' camping gas. There is also plenty of accommodation and a tourist office at Roncesvalles, about 3km N of Burguete. Roncesvalles is an important monastery on the Camino de Santiago, and the starting point for many pilgrims on the journey to Santiago de Compostella.

Facilities on Stage 4
Albergue Sorogain: tel 948 392 025 or 620 955 469 (mobile)
Hotel Loizu: tel 948 760 008 www.loizu.com
Hostal Burguete: tel 948 760 005 www.hotelburguete.com
Hostal Juandeaburre: tel 948 760 078
Camping Urrobi: tel 948 760 200 www.campingurrobi.com
Roncesvalles www.roncesvalles.es

STAGE 5

Burguete to Hiriberri (Villanueva de Aezkoa)

Start	Burguete
Distance	18km
Total Ascent/Descent	600m
Difficulty	Generally easy walking, but the descent to Orbara is steep and will be very slippery when wet. The route is complex, but the waymarking is good.
Time	4hr 45min
High Point	Ridge below Latxaga (1185m)

Until 2008 the GR11 used to go N to Roncesvalles, taking three days to reach Ochagavía via the Fábrica de Orbaiceta and the Casas de Irati; a route with little accommodation, involving a lot of road walking. It has now been replaced by a more direct two-day section to Ochagavía via Hiriberri. On Stage 5 you walk over easy wooded hills followed by a steep descent to Orbara. You get your first view of the limestone cliffs which are the major feature of the hills over the next few days.

Leave Burguete to the left of the church to reach a GR11 information board. Head ESE along a tarmac track, turn left immediately after crossing the stream and pass a picnic site. At a junction, go straight on into woods through a green gate

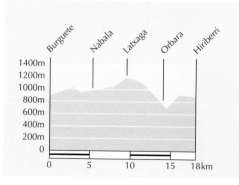

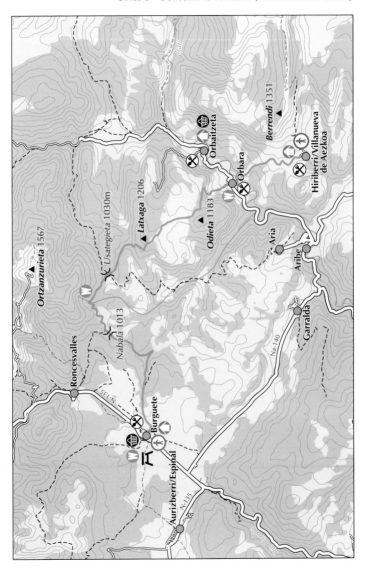

and up a rough track, heading roughly E, ignoring all turns, to a gate at the top of the wood (45min, 1035m, N42°59.255 W001°18.234). Turn left and immediately left again, heading roughly NW back into the wood. The earthen track gradually veers to the NE then left as you follow a wooded ridge, before gradually veering back to the NE to reach a saddle, **Nabala** (1hr 15min, 1013m, N43°00.069 W001°17.793). Turn right along a dirt road and ignore turns as it contours the S slopes of Ortzanzurieta (1567m). Cross a woodland stream (1hr 30min) at a cattle grid and follow the good track to a major junction at another saddle, **Usategieta** (1hr 45min, 1030m, N43°00.053 W001°16.575). Cross the cattle grid and turn right up a track climbing roughly SE through the forest. GRT-8 goes off left at Txutxurieta (2hr, 1048m) while the GR11 keeps straight on along a path. When you reach a fence with a stile, climb over and switchback up the hill, veering right well below the top, crossing some pasture to another fence.

Cross the fence, go sharp left and continue climbing to the wooded summit ridge (2hr 30min, 1185m, N42°59.420 W001°01.888) of **Latxaga** (1206m). Keep straight on, soon veering right to an open ridge. Superb dry campsites. It isn't long before you re-enter the forest and follow the waymarks

Orbara church

until you eventually reach a good track. Turn right along it, through farmland and cross a tarmac road at Aitzartea Lixarkoeta (2hr 50min, 1113m, N42°58.879 W001°15.302).

Keep straight on and soon re-enter the woods. Care is needed following the waymarks in a complex section which leads you roughly SE. Eventually you pick up an old path which winds its way downhill, finding a route through the vertical limestone cliffs above Orbara. ▶ A short section of track completes the descent to the church at **Orbara** (3hr 45min, 767m, N42°58.010 W001°14.513). Water can be obtained from the fountain just downhill from the church.

The limestone on the path will be very slippery when wet.

> Orbara is an old hamlet, with most houses having been modernised or rebuilt during Spain's building boom. There is a bar-restaurant, Eskola Taberna.

> Orbaizeta, about 30min walk (3km) along the road to the NE, is a village with a range of facilities for tourists, including Albergue Mendalitz.

Continue down the road from the church, turn right along the 'main' road then sharp left and down a concrete track. Fork left down to a bridge over the **Río Irati**. Cross the river and fork right up a grassy track which becomes a path as it takes you up the hill. When you reach a dirt road near the top of the hill, turn right along it to a saddle with a large barn at a road junction, Aldeartea (4hr 35min, 927m). Keep straight on along the tarmac road into **Hiriberri** and up a cobbled street just to the right of the church (4hr 45min, 923m, N42°56.765 W001°13.792).

> Hiriberri is another hamlet, but it does have a hostal/bar-restaurant, Hostal Alaitze, and several Casa Rural (two of which are listed below).

Facilities on Stage 5
Orbaizeta www.orbaizeta.com
Albergue Mendalitz: tel 948 766 088 www.mendilatz.com
Hostal Alaitze: tel 948 764 076 www.hostal-alaitze.com
Casa Rural Aguerre: tel 627 749 221 (mobile) www.aguerre.es
Casas Txikirrin: tel 948 764 074 www.txikirrin.com

STAGE 6
Hiriberri to Ochagavía (Otsagabia)

Start	Hiriberri
Distance	21km
Total Ascent	800m
Total Descent	1000m
Difficulty	The first 2 hours of this day are in rough limestone 'karst' terrain, after which it is easy walking along high grassy ridges. The route is complex and although the waymarking is generally good, there are some places where care will be needed with route-finding, especially in bad weather. The limestone will be slippery when wet.
Time	5hr 55min
High Point	Abodi Occidental Idorrokia (1492m), Muskilda (1071m)

The limestones cliffs of Berrendi (1351m) dominate Hiriberri. The going is rough and tough as the GR11 finds a way up through the cliffs and continues along a wooded ridge covered with limestone pavement. After this it is easy walking along the high exposed grassy ridges of the Sierra de Abodi, with sinkholes and limestone pavement to add interest. Camping above Hiriberri will have to be shared with cows and horses but then won't be feasible until you are clear of the limestone karst.

Turn left at the church, up a cobbled street and then up a concrete track to a GR11 information board at the edge of the hamlet. Head up a stony path and veer right through a gate. Follow the waymarks up stony pasture to a large concrete cattle trough where there is good water from a pipe (20min). Continue to the right of the trough, taking care to follow the waymarks as you will need to locate the path higher up the hill. This path takes you past another water-point (45min). You soon fork left up a faint path into the woods (50min, 1145m, N42°56.923 W001°12.315). This path switchbacks left and follows a slightly better path up the hill to find a gap in the crags lining the escarpment. On reaching the ridge, cross a fence and turn right (1hr 10min, 1260m, N42°57.113 W001°12.434). ◄

A faint path leads up Berrendi (1351m) to the W.

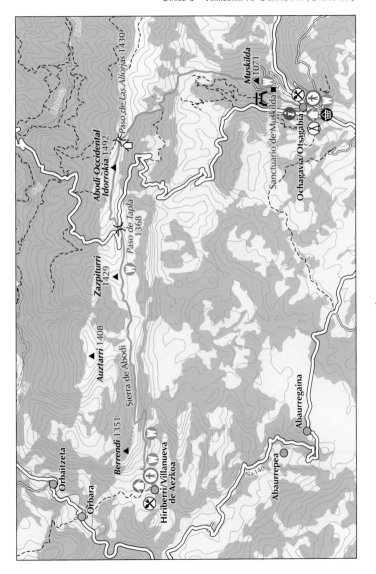

Cows below cliffs on Berrendi

Follow faint paths up the wooded ridge of **Sierra de Abodi**. This path is very rough and rocky in places. You get occasional views of the cliffs before reaching a high point of about 1400m and starting the descent. Camping is not possible on this rocky ridge. Eventually descend slightly and cross a fence into easier rough pasture (2hr), passing left of a cattle pen on the ridge. Ignore some confusing waymarking and follow the track E. There are excellent but exposed dry campsites all along the ridge. You soon fork right off the track, at a small fenced reservoir, and follow a grassy track along the ridge. Shortly after crossing a fence the track becomes a good track, which is followed past **Zazpiturri** (1429m) to reach a GR11 signpost. Just left of this sign you should be able to obtain good water where it flows into a cattle trough (2hr 55min, 1374m, N42°57.378 W001°08.827).

Continue to the **Paso de Tapla** (3hr, 1368m) where you cross a road at its highest point. Keep straight on up the

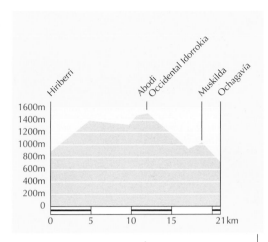

grassy ridge, picking up a rough track which switchbacks to the top of the ridge (1460m). ▶

Continue E along the grassy ridge to the main summit of **Abodi Occidental Idorrokia** (3hr 35min, 1492m, N42°57.531 W001°06.892). Keep straight on to the **Paso de Las Alforjas** (3hr 50min, 1430m, N42°57.408 W001°06.140)

From here you could climb Idorrokia (1492m), the W top of Adobi Occidental Idorrokia, to the N.

Limestone pavement on Abodi Occidental Idorrokia

where there are a number of limestone sinkholes. The old GR11 route joins from the left.

The GRT-10 and GR12 continue along the ridge, but the GR11 goes off diagonally right. You will notice a small concrete hut on your right. This 'bothy' was useable in 2013. Descend the well-marked route, keeping above the valley on your right, before descending directly down the hill to cross a fence and go down a grassy ridge to a track at the top of the forest. Turn left along the track. Good camping with possibility of water from a stream below. Soon fork right down a faint path that leads to an old path which will be slippery when wet. Eventually rejoin the track (4hr 40min, 1039m, N42°56.456 W001°04.748). Turn right and pass a barn. Last good dry camping before Ochagavía.

Continue along the grassy ridge past a shallow saddle (Urrua Xubri, 1000m) to another farm building, to reach a GR11 signpost as you enter the wood (5hr, 985m). The signpost is slightly twisted and a little confusing. The GR11 continues along the main track, climbing gently through the woods. Go straight across the tarmac road which provides road access to Muskilda and follow the track, which becomes a good path by the time it takes you over the summit of **Muskilda** (1071m) and down to the **Sanctuario de Muskilda** (5hr 25min, 1014m, N42°54.955 W001°05.116) with a water-point and well-maintained picnic site.

The shrine of **Our Lady of Muskilda** is a 12th-century Romanesque chapel that was restored in the 17th century. Inside the church is the 15th-century carved wooden image of Our Lady of Muskilda. There is a festival and pilgrimage on 8 September each year to honour the patron saint of Ochagavía.

Isolated places, such as Muskilda, were once the meeting places of covens of wizards and witches. There is evidence that the Salazarese coven met here in 1540. Salazarese is the valley occupied by Ochagavía, and the mayor of the valley was one of the participants.

The GR11 leaves the picnic area on the right to reach the far side of the Sanctuary and then follows an old cobbled path, slippery when wet, all the way to the cobbled streets of **Ochagavía**.

The GR11 comes out at the church in Ochagavía from where you drop down roughly SE, passing the supermarket to reach the misnamed medieval bridge, 'Puente Romanica' (5hr 55min, 770m, N42°54.357 W 001°05.343). The tourist office, the Fuente de Liria, some small shops and some shady seating are downstream to the right.

Ochagavía is a large village with good facilities for tourists, including a tourist office, two hostals, several Casa Rural, a supermarket and several other shops. Camping Osate at the S end of the village also has cabins, a bar-restaurant and a shop.

Facilities on Stage 6
Ochagavía Tourist Office: tel 948 890 641
Hostal Aunamendi: tel 948 890 262 www.hostalauniamendi.com
Hostal Orialde: tel 948 890 742
Camping Osate: tel 948 890 184

STAGE 7
Ochagavía to Isaba (Izaba)

Start	Ochagavía
Distance	20km
Total Ascent/Descent	700m
Difficulty	An easy day ending in a steep descent.
Time	5hr 5min
High Point	Collado de Saitsederra (1363m)

Most of the day is spent walking on good tracks through woods and along high grassy ridges before a final steep descent down woodland paths. There is little waymarking on the long sections of track, but it isn't needed. There are plenty of dry campsites throughout the route.

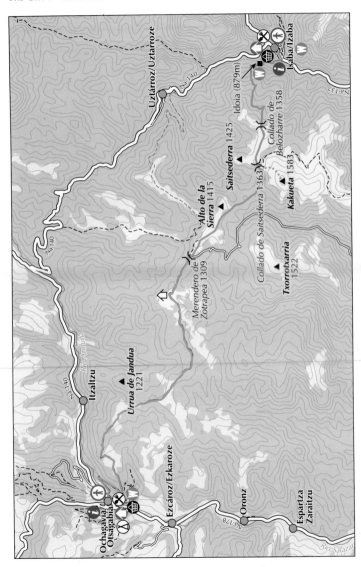

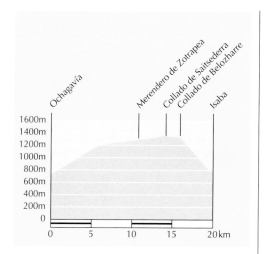

From the 'Puente Romanica' head up the **Río Anduña**, turn right across the next bridge and then immediately left to a GR11 information board. Then it's right and left up a tarmac

The misleadingly named 'Roman' bridge at Ochagavía

road, which becomes a good track after the last house. Follow this track, ignoring twists and turns, as it climbs steadily through farmland, then forest until a track joins from back right (1hr 40min, 1210m). Keep straight on, forking left 15min later and eventually passing a concrete hut at the head of the valley (2hr 20min). This was useable as a bothy in 2013. Keep going to a major junction with a GR11 sign at **Merendero de Zotrapea** (2hr 40min, 1309m, N42°53.106 W001°00.043).

Keep straight on along the middle of the three tracks ahead, soon forking right up a grassy path which rejoins the track at a shallow saddle. From here follow the track as it contours right of **Alto de la Sierra** (1415m). Ignore a major track (3hr 25min) which drops down to the right as you start contouring the N slopes of Kakueta to arrive at the **Collado de Saitsederra** (3hr 35min, 1363m, N42°51.971 W000°57.964) where the track veers sharp right. ◄

From here you could climb the grassy NE ridge of Kakueta (1583m).

There is a good view ahead of the '**whaleback' ridge** of Peña Ezkaurri (2047m), which will be the objective tomorrow.

The GR11 leaves the track and continues slightly right along a grassy ridge, veering further right then left to join a rough track which leads to the **Collado de Belozharre** (3hr 55min, 1358m, N42°51.908 W000°57.109). Turn right here, steeply down an earthen track into the woods and continue down to a signpost (4hr 5min, 1259m). You will cross some small woodland streams which may provide your first water since Ochagavía. Turn sharp left along a path which contours around the head of a valley before resuming the well-way-marked descent. Fork right at a junction (4hr 25min, 1126m) and right again at a path junction (4hr 45min, 905m) to arrive at **Idoia Dona Marialtea** (Sanctuario de Nuestra Senora de Idoia) (4hr 50min, 879m, N42°01.851 W000°55.711). ◄

This 16th-century chapel contains a 13th-century Gothic carving of the Virgin of Idoia.

Pass through a gate into the garden of the chapel which has a water-point and shady seating and would be a good place for a break before arriving in Isaba. An old cobbled path, lined with crosses, leads from the garden down to the road on the outskirts of **Isaba**. Turn left to the centre of the village (5hr 5min, 818m, N42°51.623 W000°55.434) where there is a shaded seating area next to a small park and children's play area. There is a water-point just down Calle Barrikata from here.

Isaba is a village with a tourist office (the author has never found it open!) and a good range of accommodation (some listed below). There are two supermarkets up the main road from the seating area. The larger is the best for food, but the smaller store also stocks a selection of other goods for hikers including 'original' and 'easy-clic' camping gas.

Sanctuario de Nuestra Senora de Idoia

Facilities on Stage 7
Hotel Ezkaurre: tel 948 893 303 www.hotelezkaurre.es
Hostal Onki Xin: tel 948 893 320 www.onkixin.com
Hostal Lola: tel 948 893 012 www.hostal-lola.com
Albergue Oxanea: tel 948 893 153 www.albergueoxanea.com
Pension Txiki: tel 948 893 118 www.pensiontxiki.com
Pension Txabalkua: tel 948 893 083
There are also a number of Casa Rural.

STAGE 8

Isaba to Zuriza (over Peña Ezkaurri, GR11-4)

Start	Isaba
Distance	17km; official route: 11km
Total Ascent	1400m; official route: 700m
Total Descent	1000m; official route: 200m
Difficulty	The route involves scrambling up and down broken crags on a steep limestone peak. Although the scrambling is easy, it could be intimidating for the inexperienced with a heavy rucksack. Waymarking is adequate on the wooded lower slopes and is good higher up the mountain. In wet weather the limestone will be very slippery and it might be sensible to follow the official route rather than this recommended variation. In a high snow year there may be significant snowfields on the ascent in June. The official route is easy and low-level.
Time	6hr 50min; official route: 3hr
High Point	Peña Ezkaurri (2047m); official route: Collau d'Arguibiela (1295m)
Note	Water will be a problem on this stage. The only certain water is in the Barranco Beruela, about an hour into the route.

The GR11 now leaves behind the hills of the Basque Country and enters the mountains. The GR11 used to go over the 2047m Peña Ezkaurri, but the official route now takes a shorter, low-level alternative along the Barranco de Belabarze and the old route is now official variation 11-4. This change was made because the route over Peña Ezkaurri involves easy scrambling up limestone crags and would be a demanding 'walk' in bad weather, with difficult route-finding in mist and awkward scrambling if the limestone is wet and slippery. This is the first section of the GR11 which crosses the boundary between walking and mountaineering. However, there are a number of sections in the Central Pyrenees of similar difficulty and if you can't cope with this section you will find problems further along the trail. The suggestion is that you follow the GR11-4 over Peña Ezkaurri in good weather but take the official GR11 route in bad weather.

House in Isaba

There is a 30km annual **race**, the Camille Extreme, held at the end of June, starting and finishing at Isaba. It follows the approximate route of the GR11 to Zuriza before following the GR11-4 in reverse over Peña Ezkaurri and back to Isaba.

From the seating area on the main road, fork right down Calle Barrikata, passing the water-point. Keep straight on down this street to the GR11 information board on the edge of the village. Continue along the path, past a shrine, the Ermita of Belén (Hermitage of Bethlehem), to a junction with a dirt road. Turn left to reach a road junction below the towering cliffs of the Ateas de Belabarze and Alto de Belaisaisa (30min, 883m).

The official route of the GR11 continues straight on, but our featured route (GR11-4) turns right across the

71

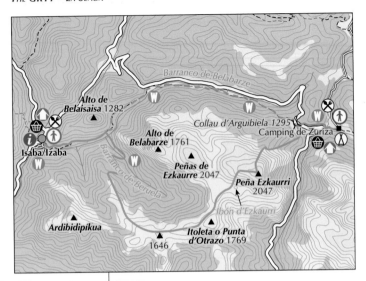

Barranco de Belabarze. The water is difficult to reach here. Continue to the roadhead (50min, 943m, N42°51.368 W000°53.436). Go right, down a rough track to cross the **Barranco de Beruela**. This stream is likely to be running well, but cows use this area so you may prefer to treat the water. Head up a possibly boggy, earthen track, switchbacking once until a small, easily missable, muddy path goes off left (1hr). Turn sharp left up this path which climbs below a fence. When the fence turns right (1hr 10min), uphill, so does the path. Continue up this small path. The waymarking and path quality improve as the path veers left across pasture (1hr 30min). This is the first good dry campsite. Continue climbing and eventually reach an open area on the ridge with a ruined stone hut (1hr 55min, 1295m, N42°50.967 W000°53.809).

The gradient now eases as you head up the ridge, through a final section of forest, to reach the grassy ridge (2hr 15min, 1395m, N42°50.671 W000°53.615). Follow the markers up the ridge, not the more prominent animal tracks which tend to contour the slopes. Veer left of **Peak 1646** to arrive back on the ridge at a shallow saddle (3hr, 1600m,

N42°50.172 W000°52.556). Exposed dry camping is possible anywhere along the ridge. Follow the ridge to another shallow saddle (3hr 20min), then veer left, contouring the NW slopes of **Itoleta o Punta d'Otrazo** (1769m). ▶

It would be easy to climb this peak from here.

Continue to a saddle (1654m) with a few trees and an electric fence. The GR11 markers first loop left of the fence, then cross and loop right, then cross again and loop left to return to the fence just W of the **Ibón d'Ezkaurri**. This shallow lake could be no more than a polluted pond or even completely dry. Go diagonally right to find a waymark at the foot of the limestone wall of Peña Ezkaurri (4hr, 1655m, N42°50.984 W000°50.955), just N of the W side of the pond. The waymarked route up the face is mainly steep, rough walking, but there are a few rocksteps to climb. The gradient eases before you reach the summit ridge (5hr 10min). There are some fairly sheltered grassy dry campsites on the plateau. Veer right up the ridge. The waymarked route passes about 50m left of the summit of **Peña Ezkaurri**, which is marked by a trig point and countless cairns (5hr 20min, 2047m, N42°51.184 W000°50.469).

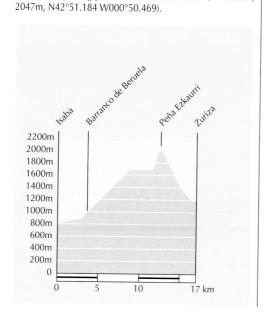

Summit plateau, Peña Ezkaurri

Return to the waymarked route and follow it roughly NNW down a well-marked path, before veering right (NE) between limestone slabs to arrive at the top of the wood (5hr 55min, 1694m, N42°51.536 W000°50.381) just above Collau d'Abizondo. This descent will be very slippery in the wet. The path continues down to the saddle then turns right, descending steeply through the woods to a road. Turn left to a sign on the brow of the hill at the **Collau d'Arguibiela** (6hr 30min, 1295m, N42°51.996 W000°49.607). ◄ Turn sharp right, following a path for about 1km before descending to the road and turning E to **Camping de Zuriza** (6hr 50min, 1227m). The entrance to this large campground is on its NE side.

The official GR11 joins from the left here.

The holiday complex at Zuriza is open all year. It includes a campground, hotel, bunkhouse, cabins, a bar-restaurant and a supermarket (not open until July) which sells 'original' camping gas. The water-point is at the far end of the buildings.

The author attempted this route in torrential rain in June 2013 and was unable to cross the Barranco de Belabarze and was forced to follow the road to Zuriza!

Official GR11 via the Valle de Belabarze

The official route of the GR11 now follows an easy low-level route along the Valle de Belabarze. It is shorter than the route over Peña Ezkaurri and with only 700m of ascent. ◄

Follow variation GR11-4 as far as the junction below the cliffs of Ateas de Belabarze and Alto de Belaisaisa (30min, 883m). Fork left and follow the good track until immediately before it swings right across the **Barranco de Belabarze** (50min).

Follow the old path up the left-hand side of the stream, ignoring a few paths to the right. As you approach the top, take the right fork and the path soon levels off in meadows. Good camping and water here and at regular intervals in the next hour. The route is not well marked, but it crosses to the S side of the stream (1hr 10min, 1015m, N42°52.475 W000°52.951) and follows the intermittent path through forest and pasture to the right of the Barranco de Belabarze. The path eventually climbs away from the stream and improves as it climbs through the forest. A track joins from back right shortly before reaching the **Collau d' Arguibiela** (2hr 40min, 1295m). The GR11 now rejoins the GR11-4, which is followed to Zuriza as described in the main route (3hr).

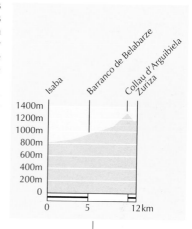

Facilities on Stage 8
Camping de Zuriza: tel 974 370 196 http://campingzuriza.valledeanso.com

Barranco de Belabarze

STAGE 9
Zuriza to La Mina

Start	Zuriza
Distance	12km
Total Ascent/Descent	800m
Difficulty	Although there are no major difficulties, care will be needed with navigation.
Time	3hr 50min
High Point	Cuello Petraficha (1964m)
Note	There are no facilities for hikers at La Mina, which gives a big problem for those who are not camping. The three 'refugios' on the route are no longer fit to use and the old refuge at La Mina is now closed. If you are not camping you need to consider your accommodation options before setting out on Stage 9: either combine Stages 9 and 10, which would mean a 10-hour day, or use the bothy at Achar d'Ayguas Tuertas, 1hr 45min into Stage 10. Alternatively, you could follow variation GR11-1 from La Mina, as described in Stage 9A, spending the night at the Hotel Usón or the other accommodation just beyond it. Stage 10 is then replaced with a two-day walk to Candanchú as described in Stage 10A and Stage 10B, staying overnight at the Refugio de Lizara.

You have now left Navarre and entered Aragón and are entering 'alpine' terrain. The limestone cliffs of the Sierra d'Alano are a magnificent sight. You can now expect to find water at regular intervals and wild camping is usually no problem. The waymarking and signposting will not always be as good as in Navarre and waymarks may be supplemented with cairns. Occasionally you will be following local routes which don't have the standard GR waymarking.

Note Fuente Fría on your left after 15min, with water welling up from underground.

Head SE along the dirt road from the campsite. ◀ Immediately before the road crosses the **Barranco Taxera** (35min, 1289m, N42°51.270 W000°47.316), fork left up the eroded path to the 'Refugio de Taxera' (1hr, 1426m, N42°51.319 W000°46.747), now a ruin. If you want to camp soon or need water, contour until you reach the Barranco Petraficha where there are plenty

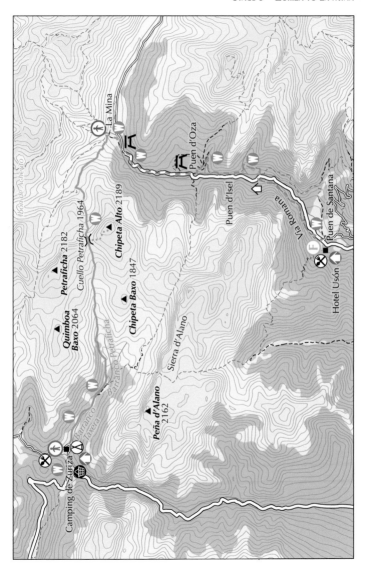

of campsites close to water, then head upstream to rejoin the GR11. Camping and water. The GR11 climbs diagonally left from the refugio and continues to climb through the forest. Fork right as the path levels, cross a stream and descend slightly to regain the **Barranco Petraficha**, which may well be dry. Follow a faint path, marked by cairns and a few waymarks, up the left-hand bank of the (dry) stream. Care will be needed to follow the path in mist.

You may well hear and possibly see your first **marmot** of the trip up this valley. You may also see your first chamois.

Pass left of a small doorless metal shed in a grassy bowl, which goes under the grand name of the Refugio de Chipeta Alto and is definitely for emergency use only (2hr). Good dry campsites. Continue E up a rocky ridge in the centre of the valley to reach the **Cuello Petraficha** (2hr 35min, 1964m, N42°51.625 W000°44.191).

It is worth climbing **Chipeta Alto** (2189m) to the SE from here. Climb the path to S before veering left up easy grass slopes to the ridge then along the grassy ridge to the summit which is a magnificent

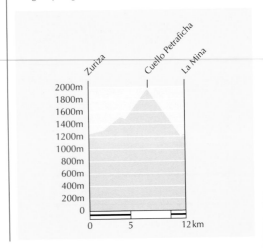

78

Sierra d'Alano

viewpoint. The summit of Chipeta Alto is an impressive rocky prow with vertical crags on its NE and SE faces (30min up, 15min down)

Don't get confused by a path contouring left, but follow the waymarks down the valley ahead. There is water from a spring after 15min. After returning to limestone terrain you reach a path junction with signpost (3hr 10min, 1545m) Turn right on a grassy shoulder and follow the path as it descends past the Refugio d'o Sabacar. In 2013 this 'bothy' was doorless with holes in the roof and well-used by animals. Descend the grassy slope SE. The official route follows a faint switchbacking path, but it's easier to head straight down the slope to reach a bridge with an old GR11 information board at **La Mina** (3hr 50min, 1230m, N42°51.311 W000°41.823).

There are no facilities at La Mina apart from streams to provide water.

STAGE 9A

Zuriza to Hotel Usón (Puen de Santana)

Start	Zuriza
Distance	22km
Total Ascent	1100m
Total Descent	1400m
Difficulty	Although there are no major difficulties, care will be needed with navigation.
Time	6hr 35min
High Point	Cuello Petraficha (1964m)
Note	This section has been ended at Hotel Usón, but you could consider alternative accommodation early on Stage 10A.

This route uses variation GR11-1 from La Mina, spending the night at the Hotel Usón or the other accommodation just beyond it. Stage 10 is then replaced with a 2-day walk to Candanchú as described in Stage 10A and Stage 10B, staying overnight at the Refugio de Lizara.

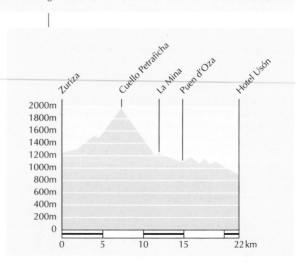

*Flock of sheep
on descent from
Cuello Petraficha*

▶ Follow Stage 9 route as far as La Mina (3hr 50min) and turn right down the dirt road, signed GR11.1 (Lizara) and GR65.3.3, a variation on the Camino de Santiago which we will follow to Hotel Usón. Cross a bridge and turn right at a picnic site and soon pass a water-point. Follow the road down the steep wooded gorge to a picnic site and youth camp at **Puen d'Oza** (4hr 30min).

For route map see Stage 9.

Don't cross the bridge but follow the GR65.3.3 signed 'Camino Viejo Puente Sil'. This was the old 'main' route (**Via Romana**) up the valley before the road was blasted out of the cliff-face. Climb, ignoring some left turns, to cross the Barranco Esparta before returning to the road at **Puen d'Isel**. Again, don't cross the bridge but continue along the GR65.3.3 on the W bank to cross Barranco Xardin and return to the river. Cross the bridge and road (5hr 40min). There is a basic bothy here that was useable in 2013.

Take the path signed 'Via Romana' and climb to the extensive remains of Lo Castiello Biello before descending easily down a good path. After crossing a stream turn left at a junction, down to the road. Turn right to a junction above **Puen de Santana**. If you don't need Hotel Usón you can turn left here and start Stage 10A. Otherwise continue down the road for about 300m and turn right up to **Hotel Usón** (6hr 35min, 896m, N42°47.392 W000°44.214).

Hotel Usón: tel 974 375 358 www.hoteluson.com

STAGE 10
La Mina to Candanchú (GR11)

Start	La Mina
Distance	22km
Total Ascent	900m
Total Descent	600m
Difficulty	The ascent is easy but there is rough terrain on the descent to the Ibón d'Estanés and Gave d'Aspe. Although this section is generally well waymarked, care will be needed with navigation on descent. The Gave d'Aspe could be difficult or impossible to cross during snow-melt or after heavy storms and an escape route via the Puerto de Somport (Col du Somport) is also described. In early season snow could make navigation on the descent to the Ibón d'Estanés difficult.
Time	6hr 30min
High Point	Col N of Punta Alta d'a Portaza (1909m)

An easy climb up a typical alpine valley is followed by a high-level 'hidden valley'. The ascent is up a valley that probably has the densest concentration of cows in the Pyrenees, which makes it difficult to find good campsites! The GR11 then pays its only visit to France as it contours on a rough path round the Gave d'Aspe before the descent to Candanchú.

If you are very lucky you might see the relatively rare Egyptian vulture in this valley.

◄ Follow the track E, soon forking right through meadows to a bridge; cross and continue past a locked cabin where you join the dirt road up the S side of the **Río Aragón Subordán**. Turn left, passing a spring fed water-point on your left (35min). Continue to the car park at the end of the public road (55min) and keep on up the track until the waymarked route shortcuts the first switchback (1hr 30min). You could avoid the steep climb by staying on the track, which switchbacks before rejoining the GR11. The path climbs steeply ESE to the unmanned refuge at **Achar d'Aguas Tuertas** where the track ends (1hr 45min, 1615m, N42°49.853 W000°37.712).

map continues on page 84

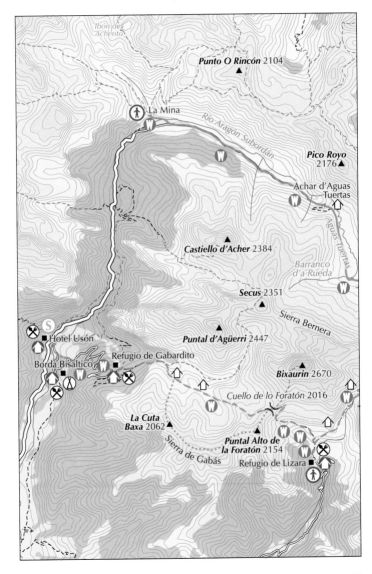

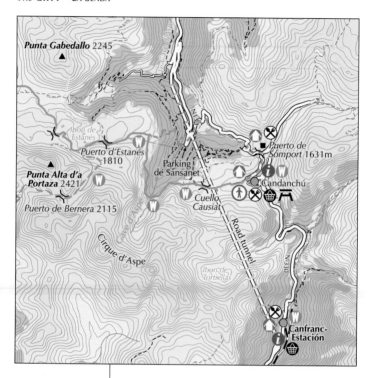

The bothy was in good condition in 2013 following major repairs in 2012.

In the Stone Age **inhabitants of these mountains** would have been hunter-gatherers, living in caves. As the climate improved and domestication of sheep, goats, cows and dogs occurred, they became nomadic livestock farmers. In the Iron Age, probably influenced by the influx of people from Central Europe, agricultural settlements started to develop in the mountain valleys.

In the meadows, just N of the hut, is one of the best preserved pre-historic **dolmens** in the Pyrenees. A burial chamber is protected by slabs of rock weighing several tonnes and would have been covered by a tumulus, a large pile of rocks and earth. Dolmens were built from the Neolithic Age until well into the Bronze Age, 3000–1500BC. During this period the inhabitants of the Pyrenees buried their dead deep within caves or within dolmens. You will also find cromlechs in these mountains, dating from about 800–300BC. These circles of stone would have contained the ashes of cremated corpses.

From the bothy, contour along a path through fallen boulders to the right of the marshy water-meadows of the **Aguas Tuertas**. The path edges down onto the flat floor of the valley and follows the path through it until you cross the **Barranco d'a Rueda** (2hr 20min, 1615m, N42°48.748 W000°37.227), possibly getting wet feet. Excellent campsites. Follow the well-waymarked path, gradually veering E, then fork right at junction marked by a post (2hr 30min) and climb to a col (3hr 20min, 1909m, N42°47.939 W000°36.245) N of Punta Alta d'a Portaza.

Water meadows at Aguas Tuertas

85

Punta Gabedallo over Ibón d'Estanés

The descent route is complex but well waymarked, as it descends, with many ups and downs, through the rocky terrain to the S of **Ibón d'Estanés** to reach the inlet at the SE tip of the lake (4hr 10min, 1787m, N42°47.856 W000°35.180). Climb E to a small pass, **Puerto d'Estanés** (1810m). Descend the left-hand side of the valley then, after 1km, veer right across a small stream. Excellent campsites. After climbing a slight rise the path immediately forks (4hr 35min, 1675m, N42°47.954 W000°34.113). ◄

Take care; this junction is frequently missed by hikers.

Escape route
If the Gave d'Aspe is likely to be uncrossable you should continue down from here following the main path to **Parking de Sansanet** in France (5hr 15min). Turn right up the main road then, after 15min, turn right up the G65-3 (Camino de Santiago), which rejoins the road just below the **Puerto de Somport** (6hr 15min) where there is the Albergue Aysa with accommodation and bar-restaurant. Turn right down the road into **Candanchú** to regain the GR11 (6hr 30min).

The GR11 forks right and contours towards the magnificent Cirque d'Aspe and enters France. Border Stone 293 is on a knoll to the left of the path. Enter the woods and traverse, with many ups and downs, below the crags and reach the

Gave d'Aspe (5hr 20min, 1560m). You will see the old higher path and the new lower path across the stream. **You must cross to the lower path as the upper path is extremely dangerous!**

Eventually you leave the woods and shortly afterwards there is a water from a pipe on the left by a signpost. Water and camping. Keep straight on, ignoring yellow/green way-marks, to reach the broad **Cuello Causiat** (6hr 5min, 1634m, N42°47.153 W000°32.853) where you re-enter Spain. The path crosses a ski piste before reaching the main ski complex at the biathlon range. Turn left down the main track and then down the road past the Alpine Military School to reach **Candanchú**. Pass Refugio Pepe Garcés and the supermarket, then head downhill past a water-point and Information Office before turning sharp right to reach Refugio-Albergues Valle de Aragón and El Aguila (6hr 30min, 1545m, N42°47.275 W000°31.758).

Candanchú is a ski resort with plenty of facilities for tourists, most of which are closed in summer! You should find several bar-restaurants open but the supermarket is only open in the high summer

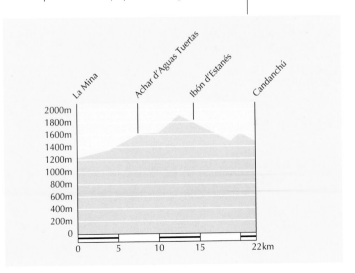

(about 15 July to 20 August). Hotels Edelweiss and Candanchú are open throughout the summer and others will be open in high summer. Refugio Pepe Garcés is open all year. Refugio-Albergues Valle de Aragón and El Aguila is open July and August. It may be open, and will open if you make a reservation in April, May, June and September.

Full tourist facilities will be open in Canfranc Estación about 5km to the S. This international railway station is a tourist resort with a good choice of hotels, hostals, albergues, Casa Rural and a good supermarket.

SNCF run a bus service from the Puerto de Somport via Candanchú and Canfranc Estación to Oloron-Ste-Marie to connect with the French rail network. There is also a local bus service from Puerto de Somport via Candanchú to Canfranc Estación and on to the much larger Jaca.

Facilities on Stage 9
Albergue Aysa: tel 974 373 023 www.albergueaysa.com
Candanchú Tourist Office:: tel 974 373 194 information@candanchu.com
Refugio Pepe Garcés: tel 974 372 378 www.refugiopepegarces.com
Refugio-Albergues Valle de Aragón and El Aguila: tel 974 373 291
    www.alberguelaguila.com
Hotel Edelweiss: tel 974 373 200 www.edelweisscandanchu.com
Hotel Candanchú: tel 974 37 30 25 www.hotelcandanchu.com
Canfranc Tourist Office: tel 974 373 141 www.canfranc.es

STAGE 10A

Hotel Usón to Refugio de Lizara (GR11-1)

Start	Hotel Usón
Distance	12km
Total Ascent	1200m
Total Descent	500m
Difficulty	Easy
Time	4hr 50min
High Point	Cuello de lo Foratón (2016m)

Stages 10A and 10B are a 2-day continuation of Stage 9A to solve the problem of no accommodation at La Mina at the end of Stage 9 for those walkers who are not camping. Stage 10A follows the GR11.1, but more importantly 'La Senda de Camille', a circuit of six huts in the Parque Natural de los Valles Occidentales in Spain and the Parque Nacional de los Pirineos in France. That route is waymarked in green/yellow and these waymarks are more numerous than the GR waymarks. You will be walking through spectacular mountain scenery and this is an excellent alternative to the main route. Look out for the very rare lammergeier, also known as the bearded vulture, which can often be seen on today's route.

▶ Return to the road junction and turn right to cross the Puen de Santana. Continue along the road until a path goes left up the hill (15min) signed 'Camino Al-Gabardito'. Continue along the road if you want Albergue Borda Bisaltico, otherwise turn left up the path which shortcuts the road up to the **Refugio de Gabardito**.

For route map see Stage 10.

> Albergue Borda Bisaltico has a hostel, campsite and bar-restaurant. Refugio de Gabardito is a modern manned refuge with full refuge facilities, open June to September.

There is a water-point at the first road crossing then you cross the road five more times before reaching the refuge (1hr 30min, 1363m, N42°47.231 W000°42.701). The water-point is slightly uphill to the right.

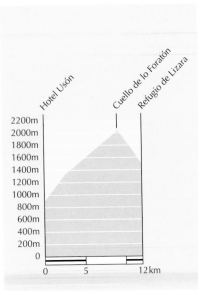

Take the track roughly E from the refuge, ignoring three left forks. The track soon becomes a good path as it climbs through spectacular limestone cliffs. Fork right at a sign (2hr) and climb to emerge above the cliffs into rolling grassland. Good campsites here and ahead. Cross a possibly dry stream and pass a small bothy, Refugio Dios Te Salbe, which was in good condition in 2013 (2hr 30min, 1550m, N42°47.050 W000°41.124). The stream by this bothy may also be dry. You soon pass another bothy, Refugio Plan d'Aniz (useable in 2013) which is above the path on the left. Cross a larger stream which is more likely to survive a dry spell and continue to **Cuello de lo Foratón** (4hr, 2016m, N42°46.617 W000°38.998).

Puntal Alto de lo Foratón

From here you could climb Puntal Alto de lo Foratón (2154m) to the SW (20min up, 15 min down). Bixaurin (2670m) to the N is also a relatively easy climb from the col. Another option is to climb La Cuta Baxa (2062m) from Refugio Dios Te Salbe, then traverse the Sierra de Gabás before descending to rejoin the route at the Cuello de lo Foratón.

The descent starts ENE before switchbacking down and passing a spring and water-point. Reach a track and follow it past another water-point, Fuente de Fuenfría, to reach a junction with a path left signed to Ibón d'Estanés. If you don't need the refuge you should turn left and start Stage 10B. Otherwise continue down to the **Refugio de Lizara** (4hr 50min, 1540m, N42°43.836 W000°38.044).

Refugio de Lizara is a modern manned refuge with full refuge facilities.

Facilities on Stage 10A
Albergue Borda Bisaltico: tel 974 375 388 www.bordabisaltico.com
Refugio de Gabardito: There is central booking for the refuges on La Senda de Camille and you can book both Gabardito and Lizara on tel 974 375 421 www.lasendadecamille.com
Refugio de Lizara: tel 974 348 433 www.refugiodelizara.com

STAGE 10B

Refugio de Lizara to Candanchú
(La Senda de Camille)

Start	Refugio de Lizara
Distance	17km
Total Ascent/Descent	800m
Difficulty	The path is clear and adequately waymarked, but you are descending a N-facing slope which will hold snow well into summer in a high snow year, making navigation a problem in mist.
Time	6hr
High Point	Puerto de Bernera (2115m)

The GR11-1 continues E from the Refugio de Lizara to reach the N-330 at Canfranc (4km S of Canfranc Estación). The recommended route follows 'La Senda de Camille' NE for a dramatic crossing of the Puerto de Bernera to rejoin the GR11 at Ibón d'Estanés.

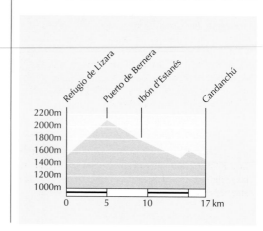

Refugio de Lizara

▸ Return to the junction and turn right, signed 'Ibón d'Estanés'. You soon pass Refugio de Ordelca (30min), a basic bothy which was useable in 2013. The path enters the Bernera valley, which is edged with impressive cliffs, and winds through the crags to the left of the Barranco de Bernera before arriving at Refugio Bernera (1hr 40min, 1967m, N42°47.015 W000°37.012). This basic bothy was useable in 2013. You soon arrive at a 'hidden valley', La Paúl de Bernera. Cross the stream and climb the right-hand side of the valley to reach the broad **Puerto de Bernera** (2hr 15min, 2115m, N42°46.946 W000°36.059).

Veer left and descend NE down the Sarrios valley, crossing the stream and veering right when the gradient increases. After losing some height, veer back left to regain the stream and follow it down to join the GR11 to the S of **Ibón d'Estanés**. Follow the GR11 down to the SE tip of the lake (3hr 40min) and on to Candanchú as described under Stage 10 (6hr).

For route map see Stage 10.

STAGE 11

*Candanchú to Sallent de Gállego
(Sallén de Galligo)*

Start	Candanchú
Distance	23km
Total Ascent	900m
Total Descent	1200m
Difficulty	There are no great difficulties in this section.
Time	6hr 35min
High Point	Ibón d'Anayet (2227m)

There are two GR11 routes from Candanchú to Sallent de Gállego. The northern route, described here, is via the Canal Roya and the Ibons d'Anayet where there are magnificent views to the Pic du Midi d'Ossau (2884m) just over the border in France. The author attempted the southern route, via the Canal d'Izás, in 2013, but soon got lost in overgrown brush with inadequate waymarking and eventually gave up! At the time of writing, there is a long road walk from the Anayet ski complex to Sallent de Gállego at the end of this stage.

From the Refugio-Albergues Valle de Aragón and El Aguila continue downhill, passing a small picnic site, before joining the main Candanchú road and then reaching a junction with the **N330** road (10min) which joins Spain to France over the Puerto de Somport. Turn left and immediately right up a tarmac track. The GR11 coincides with the well-waymarked GR65-3, a variation of the Camino de Santiago. Follow the GR65-3 waymarks (yellow arrows) as the tarmac track gives way to a track and then path before turning left along a track by a large white building. Pass the Anglasé Chimney.

> The **Anglasé Chimney** is the last surviving relic of the mining industry (silver, copper and iron), and dates back to the 16th century. There was also a factory for making combs, knives and buttons and an inn for use of cross-border travellers.

Continue to a well-signed junction (40min, 1375m, N42°46.550 W000°30.522). The GR65-3 and the variation of the GR11 via the Izás valley go off right here. Also turn right if you need to resupply in Canfranc Estación (a further 45min). There is a small basic bothy, useable in 2013, about 2min down the GR65-3. The recommended Canal Roya route continues left along the track. Soon fork left of a youth camp and, a little further on, pass the Fuente del Cerezo (55min, 1460m). Water. At a sign (1hr) the GR11 forks right along a nebulous path passing a roofless 'shelter' and continuing along the left bank of the **Río d'a Canal Roya** to a bridge (1hr 25min).

Cross and soon pass the small Refugio de Lacuas (1hr 30min, 1550m) which was just about useable in 2013. Continue, often high above the stream, gradually veering SE into the Plano d'a Rinconada and reach the lip of a flat grassy corrie (2hr 40min, 1865m) with a dolmen in the middle of it. Good camping.

It looks as if you are reaching a dead end, but follow the path up the right-hand side of the corrie heading for the

map continues on page 96

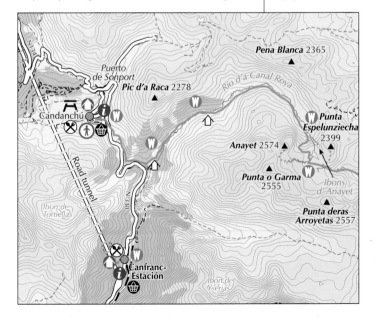

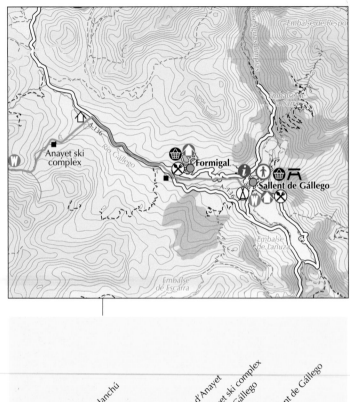

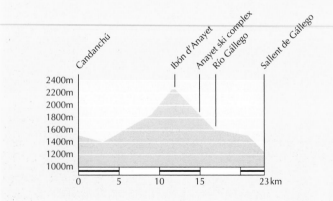

lowest crags. The path is well cairned with occasional way-marks. The path crosses a stream and then switchbacks easily through the crags to emerge at the top (3hr 50min, 2225m, N42°46.775 W000°26.818). Now head E and you arrive at the **Ibón d'Anayet**. Good campsites. There is a second smaller lake to the N which is better for swimming, if it isn't covered in ice as it was in mid-July 2013! ▸

The impressive mountain to the N, in France, is the Pic du Midi d'Ossau, probably the most photographed mountain in the Pyrenees.

It would be possible to climb **Anayet** (2574m) by its SW ridge from the Cuello d'Anayet (2413m). An easier peak is Punta Espelunziecha (2399m) to the E of the lakes, which can be climbed by its S ridge (30min up, 15min down).

The GR11 skirts the right-hand edge of the meadow to the S of the Ibón d'Anayet and over grassy moraine to reach the top of the descent. This could be confusing in mist as there are old paths and waymarks, but if in doubt keep close to the left bank of Barranco Anayet. Further down, the path crosses the stream several times before arriving at the **Anayet ski complex** (5hr, 1747m, N42°46.770 W000°24.798). ▸

There are no waymarks until you reach the Rio Gállego below Formigal. Look out for new signs and waymarking as this is a section of the GR11 which would benefit from rerouting to avoid the road walking.

Pic du Midi d'Ossau from Ibon d'Anayet

Walk down the ski road, which is closed to traffic in summer, to reach the car park on the main **A-136** road (5hr 25min, 1550m). The small bothy attached to the farm buildings at the car park was useable in 2013. Turn right down the main road. It is safest to walk on the left-hand hard shoulder. Fork right at a roundabout. You could visit the ski resort of Formigal, but Sallent de Gállego has more character and provides everything the walker is likely to need. Pass a petrol station with bar-restaurant and very small shop. 400m later (5hr 55min), just before the bridge over the **Río Gállego**, turn left down a waymarked track and follow it to the outskirts of **Sallent de Gállego**. The road on your left as you descend is the old main road, C-136, joining the ski resort of Formigal to Sallent de Gállego. Cross the C-136 on the outskirts of Sallent de Gállego and take the next turn left downhill to a tiny park with seats and a water-point at the top of the town centre. The Gorgol Free Mountain equipment store is right from here. From the park, continue through the town to the main square with water-point (6hr 35min, 1294m, N42°46.336 W000°19.874).

Sallent de Gállego is a small town with at least 12 hotels, a selection of bar-restaurants and shops, and a municipal campground with basic facilities at the NE end of the town. Gorgol Free Mountain stocks 'Coleman-style' camping gas.

Facilities on Stage 11
Sallent de Gállego Tourist Office: tel 974 488 012 www.sallent.info
Hotel Balaitús: tel 974 488 059 www.hotelbalaitus.com
Hotel Bocalé: tel 974 488 555 www.bocale.com
Hostal Centro: tel 974 488 019 www.hostalcentrosallent.com
Gorgol Free Mountain www.gorgol.com

STAGE 12

Sallent de Gállego to Refugio de Respomuso

Start	Sallent de Gállego
Distance	12km
Total Ascent	900m
Total Descent	100m
Difficulty	Easy
Time	3hr 50min
High Point	Refugio de Respomuso (2220m)
Note	If you do not need the Refugio de Respomuso it is easier and slightly shorter to take the old route of the GR11 along the S shore of the Ibón de Respomuso.

This is only a short stage, but it leaves you in position to climb the Cuello de Tebarrai and Cuello de l'Infierno in the morning on the following day, which is safer as you would not want to be caught on these high passes in an afternoon thunderstorm. You are entering a region of granite mountains which provides much of the most spectacular scenery in the Pyrenees.

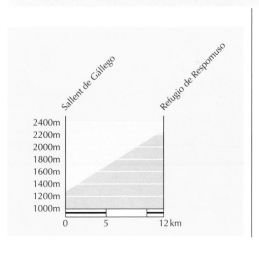

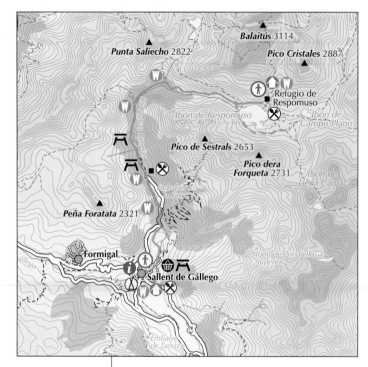

Leave the main square on the left (NE corner) and head out of
town on streets just left of the stream, then follow a signed path
along the river bank to a bridge. In 2013 there was a confusing
sign on the bridge which you should ignore – just continue
up the track on the left bank of the stream. Turn left at a well-
signed junction and follow an old walled path up to a road
(35min). Turn right, forking left just before the dam (45min,
1438m). Water-point. Follow the path along the SW shore of
the **Embalse de la Serra** to arrive at the N end of the reservoir
(55min, 1438m). On your right is Bar-restaurante Asador de
la Sarra with a picnic area, open covered shelter, water-point
and car park. Continue up the excellent path past the Plana
Tornadizas, a recreational area with picnic table. Discrete
camping would be possible here. You won't find many camping opportunities until after the Refugio de Respomuso.

Now climb up a wooded gorge, often high above the Rio Agua Limpias. Ignore a path left signed to Collado la Soba (1hr 50min) shortly before the gorge narrows at the Paso de l'Onso (1700m). The path follows a ledge along the cliff face, but this is a 'tourist' path and the edge is guarded by a fence. The path veers E, passing another left turn signed to Ibones de Arriel (2hr 15min) which you ignore, and you climb a long V-shaped valley through a granite landscape. Fork left as you approach the dam to reach a signpost (3hr 35min, 2160m, N42°49.029 W000°17.739) just NW of the **Ibón de Respomuso**.

GR11 hikers on the climb to Respomuso

If you don't need to visit the Refugio de Respomuso you are best to follow the old route of the GR11 from here which goes right down to the (locked) Capella de la Virgin de las Nieves, crosses the dam and continues above the S bank of the reservoir.

The GR11 goes straight on for a short distance before forking left and switchbacking up the slope, then contouring well above the N bank of the reservoir and forking right to the **Refugio de Respomuso** (3hr 50min, 2220m, N42°49.010 W000°17.267). There is no camping by the refuge, but there are plenty of good campsites above the E shore of the reservoir and up to the Ibón de Llena Cantal.

The Refugio de Respomuso is a large modern manned refuge with normal refuge facilities. It is open all year but can be very busy at weekends in the summer as it is the base for the climb of Balaitús (3144m) to the N.

Facilities on Stage 12
Refugio de Respomuso: tel 974 337 556

STAGE 13
Refugio de Respomuso to Baños de Panticosa

Start	Refugio de Respomuso
Distance	13km
Total Ascent	700m
Total Descent	1300m
Difficulty	This is possibly the most difficult stage on the GR11, with an ascent up a very steep gully to the Cuello de Tebarrai and steep descents from here and from the Cuello de l'Infierno. There is a lot of boulderfield to cross and there will be snow on the route in early season and possibly well into summer. It is advisable to get over the pass in the morning as it would be dangerous to be caught in an afternoon thunderstorm while crossing the passes.
Time	6hr 10min
High Point	Cuello de Tebarrai (Piedrafita) (2765m), Cuello de l'Infierno (2721m)

The route passes through superb alpine scenery. The Cuello de Tebarrai is not only the highest col on the GR11, it is also the most demanding. This is not a route for the inexperienced in poor weather or in early season.

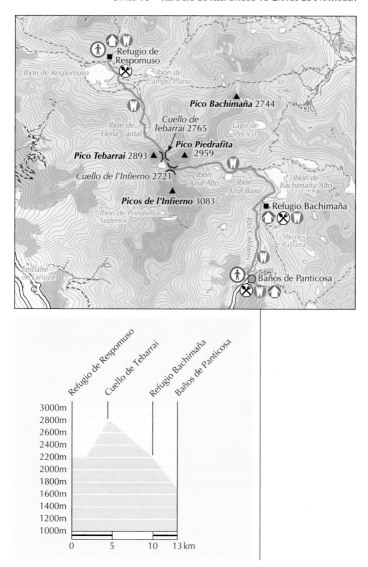

103

Pico Tebarrai above Ibón de Tebarrai

Follow waymarks SE from the Refugio de Respomuso, past the old refuge which is now locked. The route is not well waymarked as you continue roughly SE, aiming for the E tip of the reservoir, and then head S to pick up the clear path which goes round the S shore of the reservoir. This is where the old route above the S shore of the reservoir rejoins the GR11. Turn left and, immediately before the stream draining the Llena Cantal valley, turn right along a faint waymarked path (40min, 2140m, N42°48.624 W000°16.817). The path crosses the stream twice before veering away from it to reach **Ibón de Llena Cantal** (1hr 35min, 2438m, N42°48.002 W000°16.441). The campsites on the E shore of this lake are the last comfortable sites until the Ibón Azul Alto.

The path follows the W shore of the lake before veering left up a rocky ridge and following a stable path up the moraine. The climb was largely free of snow in early July 2012, but in mid-July 2013 there was continuous snow down to the lake! You appear to be heading for a dead end below the cliffs, but you veer right up an uncomfortably steep gully. Take care not to dislodge stones on to those below. You arrive at a rocky notch in the ridge, the **Cuello de Tebarrai** (2hr 50min, 2765m, N42°47.527 W000°16.004). ◄

The rocky E ridge of Pico Tebarrai (2893m) is an easy climb from here.

A short unpleasant descent on the other side leads to a path contouring left across moraine above the Ibón de Tebarrai to the **Cuello de l'Infierno** (3hr 5min, 2721m). ▸

There is a popular climb of the Picos de l'Infierno (3083m) from here but it involves exposed scrambling.

Descend the well-waymarked route, where snow tends to linger well into summer. The route crosses the stream twice before passing left of the **Ibón Azul Alto** (3hr 35min). This lake has the first good campsites on the descent. Climb a little before descending to the dam of the Ibón Azul Baxo (3hr 50min, 2360m, N42°47.300 W000°14.464). The way-marked path crosses the outlet stream and recrosses to descend to the left of the stream. It could be easier to stay left of the stream. Reach a flat grassy area (4hr 10min) with a signpost just above the large **Ibón de Bachimaña Alto** reservoir. Turn right across the stream and follow the path which traverses up and down high above the W bank of the reservoir to reach the dam of the Ibón Baxo de Bachimaña (4hr 45min). From here it is 200m to the **Refugio Bachimaña** (2200m, N42°46.786 W000°13.658).

Refugio Bachimaña is a large, modern manned refuge, opened in July 2012, offering a full refuge service. It is open all year.

Waterfall on Río Calderés

From the refuge return to the dam and follow the well-marked path down the right-hand side of the **Río Calderés** which flows down a beautiful granite valley. You pass a flat grassy area beside the stream (5hr 35min). The last camping before Baños de Panticosa. Ignore bridges to the left as you continue down the right-hand side of the stream to reach the Refugio Casa de Piedra on the edge of **Baños de Panticosa** (6hr 10min, 1636m, N42°45.744 W000°14.015). The water-point is outside the Hotel Continental.

Baños de Panticosa is a 'thermal spa' resort catering for those with big budgets. Fortunately, there is a refuge, Refugio Casa de Piedra, which has a full refuge service and is open all year, as well as the 5-star Gran Hotel (with casino) and the new 4-star Hotel Continental. There is also a café, bar and restaurant, but only a souvenir shop.

Facilities on Stage 13
Refugio Bachimaña: tel 697 126 967Refugio Casa de Piedra: tel 974 487 571
Hotel Continental: tel 974 487 161 www.panticosa.com

STAGE 14
Baños de Panticosa to San Nicolás de Bujaruelo (Buxargüelo)

Start	Baños de Panticosa
Distance	21km
Total Ascent	1100m
Total Descent	1400m
Difficulty	There are fairly long sections of boulderfield on this stage. Some of the waymarks were getting rather faded in 2013, but are supplemented by plenty of cairns. The crossing of the Río Ara could be difficult in snowmelt or in wet weather.
Time	7hr 5min
High Point	Cuello de Brazato (2566m)

The crossing of the Cuello de Brazato, another spectacular alpine pass, would be rather daunting for the inexperienced in bad weather.

Head into Baños de Panticosa from the refuge and leave up the steps to the left of the Restaurante la Fontana at the E of the resort. Turn left along a track and then, at a switchback, keep straight on along a good path. This well-graded path is in shade if you make an early morning start. You should ignore any paths coming up from the left to reach a pipeline

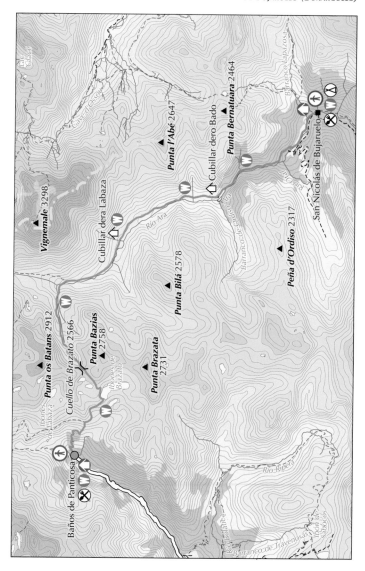

(1hr 40min, 2206m). Dry camping to the right. Now follow a well-cairned path NE up a boulderfield, then veer right (SE) to reach the dam of the **Ibón dero Brazato** (2hr 20min, 2380m, N42°45.149 W000°12.751). This is your first water on the climb.

Veer left along the N shore of the reservoir and then follow the path as it switchbacks N to reach the W shoulder of Pico de Baziás (2hr 45min). The GR11 now contours across a boulderfield to reach **Cuello de Brazato** (Puerto Biello) (3hr 10min, 2566m, N42°45.464 W000°12.106).

Follow the small path NE down the valley, passing left of the Ibons deros Batanes on boulderfields. Cross the outlet of the third tarn and continue on easier terrain to a grassy area (4hr). The first good campsites in this section. Cross the stream and continue descending the left bank, recrossing lower down to reach the **Río Ara** (4hr 25min, 2000m, N42°45.988 W000°10.226). This river could be awkward to cross during snowmelt or after rain. It is safer to cross about 100m further downstream where there is a slight levelling off of the river. ◄

Don't be afraid to get your feet wet; it's safer than boulder-hopping.

Continue down the left-hand side of the river to a small hut, **Cubillar dera Labaza** (5hr 10min). This bothy was

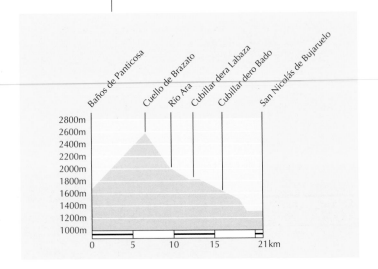

useable in 2013, but in need of repairs. You are now in cow country and good campsites are in short supply. Continue down the left-hand bank to **Cubillar dero Bado** (6hr 5min), a small bothy which was useable in 2013. Follow a track from here down the left-hand side of the valley, turning sharp left at a junction (6hr 45min) and pass through a delightful grassy area beside the river. No camping. You soon reach the medieval bridge at **San Nicolás de Bujaruelo** (7hr 5min, 1338m). The Refugio de Bujaruelo with campground and car park is across the bridge.

Australian GR11 hikers beside Ibón dera Brazato

> Refugio de Bujaruelo has full refuge facilities and is open from about 1 March to 2 November. The campground is open June–September.

Facilities on Stage 14
Refugio de Bujaruelo: tel 974 486 412 www.refugiodebujaruelo.com

STAGE 15
San Nicolás de Bujaruelo to Refugio de Góriz

Start	San Nicolás de Bujaruelo
Distance	24km
Total Ascent	1600m
Total Descent	800m
Difficulty	In this section you are back onto tracks and good paths. The GR11 is well signed and waymarked.
Time	7hr 35min
High Point	Refugio de Góriz (2160m)
Note	Camping is not allowed in the National Park except at the official campgrounds in the valleys. The regulations allow you to bivouac, with or without tent, above 2100m in the Ordesa Sector, which includes the Refugio de Góriz, and 1800m in the Añisclo Sector, which covers the canyons of Stage 16. Camping is only permitted using small tents between the hours of sunset and sunrise and tents must not be left up during the day. Effectively this means there is no wild camping in this section except at the Refugio de Góriz where there is a designated camping area. www.ordesa.net

This walk takes you down the canyon of the Garganta de Bujaruelo and up the world-renowned Ordesa Canyon through some of the most magnificent scenery of the Pyrenees. You are in the Parque National de Ordesa y Monte Perdido and will have to share the canyon with thousands of tourists.

A busy dirt road continues down from the refuge to the Puen deros Nabarros, but fortunately the GR11 is now routed along paths along the opposite side of the river to the road. Stay on the E side of the **Río Ara** and follow the path along the left-hand bank of the river. Pass a bridge (45min) with a sign to **Camping Valle de Bujaruelo** which is just across river.

Camping Valle de Bujaruelo has a bunkhouse, cabins, bar-restaurant and small supermarket in

Puente de Bujaruelo

addition to camping. The shop stocks the 'original' camping gas.

Continue down the left bank of the river to **Puen de Santa Elena** (1hr). Here the dirt road crosses the river, and so do we. Don't be tempted to follow the road as you will miss a spectacular path following ledges along cliff faces high above the river. Turn left after crossing the bridge. At one point a path joins from back right and further on you fork left (1hr 35min). ▶

The right turn would take you down to San Antón and Torla.

Torla is a tourist village with supermarkets, bar-restaurants, a large number of hotels, hostals, refugios and Casa Rural as well as three campgrounds (listed below). There are buses from Torla into the Ordesa Canyon every 15–30min. There are several good outdoor stores. Intersport stocks 'original', 'easy-clic' and 'Coleman-style' camping gas.

Continue down to the road and turn left. In a few minutes fork left across the old bridge at **Puen deros Nabarros** (1hr 50min, 1060m, N42°39.176 W000°06135).

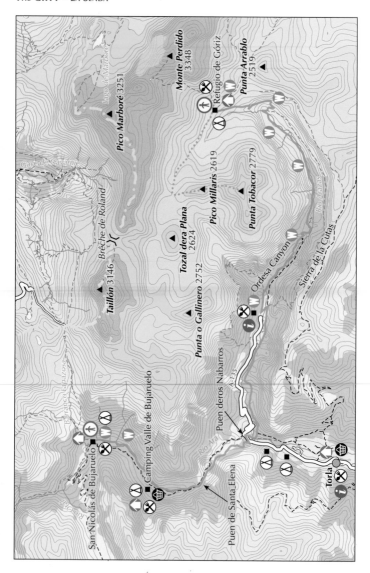

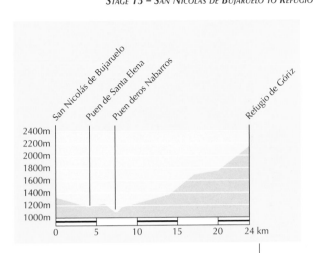

Turn right under the N end of the new bridge and descend to cross the **Río Arazas** on a concrete bridge over some huge but inaccessible swimming holes. Shortly afterwards turn sharp left, uphill, then left at another junction. Both right turns lead to Torla. You now climb steadily past an open shelter and fork right past a viewpoint to the Cascade de Tamborrotera. ▸ Continue past a turn to the Cascade de Abetos viewpoint. The next fork left, which you also ignore, is to a bridge with a monument to Lucien Briet.

If you visit the viewpoint you can rejoin the GR11 higher up.

Frenchman **Lucien Briet** first visited Ordesa in 1891 and was captivated by its outstanding beauty and realised the need to protect the area. He helped promote the cause, which resulted in the creation of the Parque National de Ordesa y Monte Perdido in 1918.

Ignore the next bridge as well, unless you want to visit the bar-restaurant at the roadhead on the opposite side of the river. The GR11 continues on a track along the floor of the valley to reach a path which has been designed for wheelchairs. Turn left along it, crossing a bridge and reaching the National Park Information Office at the top of a huge car park (3hr 25min, 1320m). There are toilets and a water-point

*Waterfalls in the
Ordesa Canyon*

beside the information centre and a bar-restaurant at the W
end of the car park.

Turn right up the track, forking right at a monument, and
climb steadily through the woods. Pass a viewpoint for the
Cascada de Arripas with a water-point (4hr). If you just continue up the GR11 along the main path, ignoring the viewpoints, you will miss what is probably the most spectacular
waterfall in the Pyrenees. Instead follow the sign to Cascada
de la Cueva and Cascada del Estrecho. After visiting the
Cueva viewpoint continue up the path to a viewpoint at the
bottom of Cascada del Estrecho. Then continue up the path
to rejoin the GR11. Almost immediately there is an unsigned

path forking right to a viewpoint a little below the top of the Cascada del Estrecho. Rejoin the GR11 and soon reach the final two viewpoints for the Cascada del Estrecho.

Continue past another open shelter (4hr 30min). Eventually the gradient eases at another cascade, Gradas de Soasa (5hr 10min, 1650m), where you pass another water-point and the track becomes a 'tourist' path. After a little more climb, you reach the grassy 'hidden valley' of the Circo de Soasa (5hr 25min, 1700m). Pass a small bothy which is intended for emergency use only and continue to the new bridge at the foot of the Cascada de Caballo ('horse-tail falls') (5hr 50min, 1760m, N42°39.005 E000°00.932). You have now crossed the Greenwich Meridian! This is where the 'tour-ist' path ends and you are back onto normal mountain paths.

> There is a signed shortcut by which the adventurous can climb the **lower band of crags** on iron rods (*las clavijas*) found in the obvious cave to the right of the falls. The author has not checked this route but is informed by the guardians of the Refugio de Góriz that it is easy.

The walker will cross the bridge and take the lower path, signed to Refugio de Góriz, forking left to climb through

Ordesa Canyon seen from below Refugio de Góriz

the first band of crags. Contour left, crossing a small stream (good water, 6hr 25min), before climbing through the second band of crags and continuing easily to **Refugio de Góriz** (7hr 35min, 2160m, N42°39.795 E000°00.909).

The Refugio de Góriz has a full refuge service. There is an area to the SE of the refuge where overnight camping is permitted. Please use the toilets outside the refuge. The refuge offers meals and picnic boxes to campers. You may not leave your tent up during the day, but if you want to explore the fantastic area around the refuge it is possible to leave your camping equipment in a locker.

The **classic day trip** from Refugio de Góriz would be the climb of Monte Perdido (3348m), which is spectacular but relatively easy for properly equipped, experienced mountaineers. It is not a route for the casual walker. Equally spectacular, but rather easier, is the climb to the well-known col, Brêche de Roland (Breca Rolán), from where you can climb Taillón (Punta Negra) (3146m). If you want an easier summit you could climb Punta Tobacor (2779m) via Collado Millaris and Pico Millaris (2619m).

Facilities on Stage 15
Camping Valle de Bujaruelo: tel 974 486 161
    www.campingvalledebujaruelo.com
Torla Tourist Office: tel 974 486 378 www.torla.es
Hostal Alto Aragón: tel 974 486 172
Hotel Ordesa: tel 974 486 125 www.hotelordesa.com
Refugio Lucien Briet: tel 974 486 221 www.refugiolucienbriet.com
Refugio L'Atalaya: tel 974 486 022 www.refugiorestauranteatalaya.com
Camping Río Ara has a shop and bar-restaurant. Tel 974 486 248
    www.campingrioara.com
Camping San Antón has cabins. Tel 974 486 063
Camping Ordesa has cabins, bar-restaurant and shop. Tel 974 117 721
    www.campingordesa.es
Refugio de Góriz: tel 974 341 201 www.goriz.es

STAGE 16

Refugio de Góriz to Refugio de Pineto

Start	Refugio de Góriz
Distance	13km; old GR11:12km
Total Ascent	1000m; old GR11: 800m
Total Descent	2000m; old GR11: 1800m
Difficulty	The descent from Collado Arrablo to the Río Bellos is tough and, although not technically difficult, requires great care. When wet, it will be slippery climbing down rocksteps as the path finds a way down the bands of limestone crags lining the canyon containing the Barranco Arrablo. Crossing the Barranco Arrablo could be awkward in snowmelt or after heavy rain. The 1000m descent from Collata Añisclo is unpleasantly steep and is mentally as well as physically tiring requiring continuous concentration. You should not attempt this descent if there is snow on the route. Those of a nervous disposition will probably find that this descent takes considerably longer than suggested below. The old GR11 is difficult and exposed, but waymarking is excellent.
Time	6hr 50min; old GR11: 6hr 10min
High Point	Collata Arrablo (2343m), Collata Añisclo (2453m)
Note	The contours in Valle Bellos on the base map were not accurate, and although they have been adjusted by the author they should not be relied on for navigation.

The GR11 used to make its way round the S side of Punta las Olas via ledges and gullies, but this route is dangerous in snow and has now been replaced by the described route. If you want to attempt the old route, which is described as an alternative below, you should check its condition at the Refugio de Góriz – do not attempt it unless you have confirmed that it is free of snow. The lower route followed by the GR11 is still a tough and spectacular route.

The GR11 goes SE from the refuge, passing to the left of the weather station and following a well-marked path to **Collata Arrablo** (40min, 2343m, N42°39.265 E000°01.941). ▶

You can climb Punta Arrablo (2519m) from here.

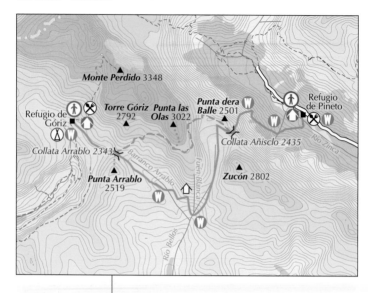

The old route of the GR11 goes off left from here. The GR11 follows the path SE, down-climbing a number of easy rocksteps to reach the **Barranco Arrablo** (1hr 30min, 2329m).

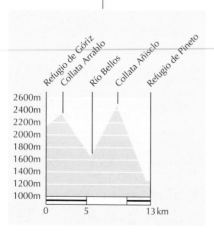

Cross, probably getting wet feet, and follow the path on the other side. As you veer left, notice **Fuén Blanca**, the waterfall on your left which flows from under the limestone crags of the Punta las Olas. Continue descending past a tiny stone bothy, which was in useable condition in 2012, and down to a bridge over the **Río Bellos** (2hr, 1660m).

Cross, turn left and climb steadily with occasional easy rocksteps before crossing a stream (2hr 50min). Last water on the ascent. As you approach the headwall of the canyon, veer right (roughly E). Excellent,

Youth group on descent from Collata Arrablo

probably dry, campsites. Continue to the **Collata Añisclo** (4hr 20min, 2453m, N42°39.616 E000°04.572) where the alternative route rejoins the GR11.

The descent ahead, down a steep rocky slope, looks very intimidating and it would be dangerous to descend without the well-waymarked path. Follow the waymarks carefully! After an hour you reach piped water from a small spring on a grassy ridge by a Parque Nacional sign (5hr 20min). There is space for two small tents here. Shortly afterwards, turn right. The difficulty continues as you descend through the woods with a number of awkward rocksteps to climb down. Water isn't a problem as you cross several streams before reaching a junction at the bottom of the descent (6hr 40min). If you don't need to visit the Refugio de Pineta you can start the Stage 17 route which returns to this point. Otherwise, turn right and cross the flood plain of the **Río Zinca**, probably getting wet feet, following cairns and yellow waymarks to reach the **Refugio de Pineta** (6hr 50min, 1240m) which is on the A-2611 road.

Refugio de Pineta has full refuge services.

Alternative via the old route of GR11

This route is not technically any more difficult than the new GR11, but it is much more exposed and potentially more dangerous. From **Collata Arrablo** (40min) turn left, climbing roughly NE. The waymarks and cairns are rather sparse at first, but excellent higher up. Cross a stream (1hr 20min) and veer right then left to reach about 2600m. The route now veers E, climbing gently to reach 2700m (2hr 10min) on the SE ridge of Punta las Olas before starting to contour easily round the ridge.

A cairned route goes off left (2hr 25min) and gives a reasonably easy climb of **Punta las Olas** (3022m).

Refugio de Góriz · Collata Arrablo · Collata Añisclo · Refugio de Pineto

2800m
2600m
2400m
2200m
2000m
1800m
1600m
1400m
1200m
1000m

0   5   12 km

Descent route from Collata Añisclo

The route continues to reach the E face of the ridge where you pass a small stream flowing out of the rockwall (2hr 40min). Almost immediately you reach the start of the difficult section. Chains add security as you scramble up a gully and then are essential as you make a strenuous pull up a small rockstep. Chains again provide necessary security on an exposed descent of smooth limestone slabs. The going then eases on a gradual descent to the Collata deras Solas (3hr 30min). Do not descend here. The route climbs slightly, skirting Punta dera Balle, before descending to **Collata Añisclo** (3hr 40min, 2453m, N42°39.616 E000°04.572) where you rejoin the main variation of the GR11 and descend to the Refugio de Pineta (6hr 10min).

Facilities on Stage 16
Refugio de Pineta: tel 974 501 203 www.refugiopineta.com

STAGE 17
Refugio de Pineto to Parzán

Start	Refugio de Pineto
Distance	21km
Total Ascent	1000m
Total Descent	1200m
Difficulty	This easy mountain section is poorly waymarked.
Time	6hr 5min
High Point	Collata las Coronetas (2159m)

This section pales into insignificance compared with the previous few days, but it is still a fine walk with superb views back to the Circo de Pineta. The descent down Río Real valley is down a dirt road.

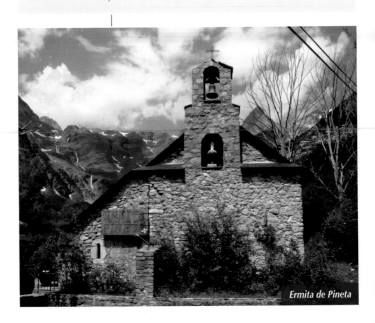

Ermita de Pineta

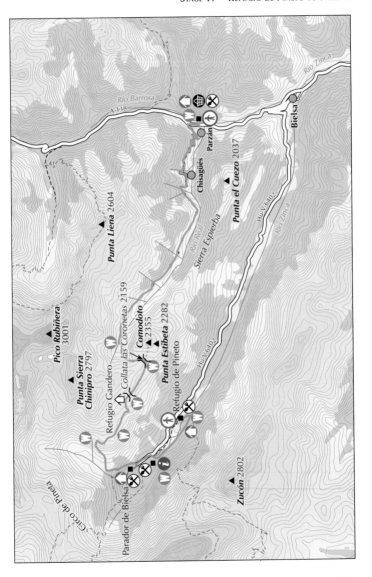

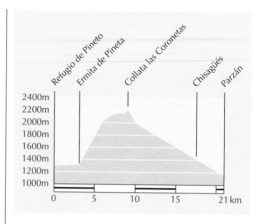

It would be possible to walk up the road to the Ermita de Nuestra Senora de Pineta, but the route of the GR11 up the S bank of the Río Zinca is much more pleasant. Return from the Refugio de Pineto to the path junction on the S bank of the **Río Zinca** and turn right along the foot of some crags. Continue through meadows and woodland on the floor of the valley, eventually arriving at a large car park with water-point and National Park Information Office. There is a bar-restaurant in high season (mid-July to late August). No camping.

Cross the bridge at the S end of the car park and turn left, up the road, passing a youth camp before reaching the Ermita de Nuestra Senora de Pineta (45min, 1290m), immediately before the **Parador de Bielsa Hotel**. Fuen Santa, at the chapel, was dry in 2013.

Follow the path to the right of the chapel, signed to Llanos de Larri, and ignore many smaller paths as you climb through the woods to a good track. You could turn right up this track, but the GR11 shortcuts the switchbacks before following it to reach the open pasture of La Larri. You soon see a farm building on your right (1hr 30min, 1560m, N42°41.148 E000°05.130). There are no signs or waymarks but you should turn right (ENE) past it and cross pasture, heading for the path you can see up the right-hand side of a (dry) streambed above you.

Follow the path, veering left at a yellow sign painted onto a boulder. Continue NE until you almost reach the

Barranco las Opacas, then switchback up the hill. When you see an open area on your left, where you may find water, the path veers right (S) (2hr 25min) and then left as it leaves the forest and heads up a grassy valley. Climb out of the valley on the right to reach the open pasture of the Plana es Corders. The path is rather indistinct but it can be followed past a cattle trough with accessible spring-fed water.

Continue SE to a track. If you are still on the GR11 you will see the 'path' continue across the track. If, as is more likely, you have lost the GR11, turn left up the track which switchbacks to a reliable spring, Fuen de la Plata. Just above the spring is the **Refugio Gandero** (3hr 10min, 2100m, N42°41.010 E000°06.393), a bothy which was useable in 2013. Continue E to where the GR11 joins the track as it crosses a low ridge, Collateta Plana Fonda (2103m).

Follow the track down into a long grassy bowl, the Plana Fonda, passing another cattle trough with accessible spring water (3hr 25min). Water and good camping. Shortly afterwards veer left, following waymarks, uphill to the **Collata las Coronetas** (Collado de Pietramula) (3hr 45min, 2159m, N42°40.533 E000°07.412). This isn't the conspicuous V-shaped col at the head of the Plana Fonda, but the low point on a grassy ridge further left. ▶

From here you could make an easy ascent of Comodoto (2355m) to the E of the col by its W ridge (30min up, 20min down).

Punta Sierra Chinipro from Comodoto

Descend just left of the dry valley, veering right through some large boulders which have fallen from the N face of Comodoto. The last good camping on the descent. Continue down to the bridge over the Barranco Pietramula (4hr 10min, 1907m, N42°40.949 E000°07.777). Cross and turn right down the dirt road. There is frequent water and camping is possible in several places on the descent. The dirt road becomes a tarmac road shortly before **Chisagüés** (5hr 30min, 1380m).

> **Chisagüés** was the base for iron and silver mines dating back to the 12th century. Mining reached its peak in the 16th century, when five foundries were working in the valley, and continued until the mid-20th century.

Continue down the road, ignoring a tarmac road going sharp right to a farm. Just after this junction there is a GR11 sign forking left (6hr, N42°39.754 E000°12.578). This is the route to take at the start of the next stage, but you will almost certainly want to continue down to visit the facilities at **Parzán**. The facilities aren't actually in the hamlet of Parzán but on the main road, so you should continue down to the main road and turn right to the service area (6hr 5min, 1144m).

> **Parzán** is another old mining village with mines dating back to the 11th century. The village was completely destroyed in 1936 during the Spanish Civil War, but has been rebuilt.

> The petrol station at Parzán has a bar-restaurant and small supermarket. Hostal la Fuen, which also has a bar-restaurant, is a little further down on the right. A large new supermarket was being built in 2013.

Facilities on Stage 17
Parador de Bielsa Hotel: tel 974 501 011
Hostal la Fuen: tel 974 501 047 www.lafuen.com

STAGE 18

Parzán to Refugio de Biadós (Viadós)

Start	Parzán
Distance	22km
Total Ascent	1500m
Total Descent	900m
Difficulty	This is an easy day with much of the route being on tracks. Adequate, but infrequent, waymarking.
Time	6hr 10min
High Point	Collata Chistau (2346m)

The climb is rather uninteresting, but the descent is through very scenic terrain.

Return up the road towards Chisagüés and, just after the first bend, turn right along the track with a GR11 sign. You soon fork left up a small path, signed to Ordizeto, and climb onto the flat concrete top of a water pipeline. Turn right along it, cross a concrete water channel and veer right then left

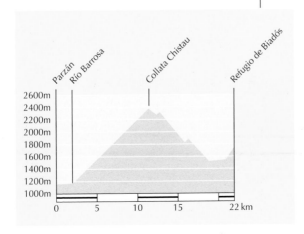

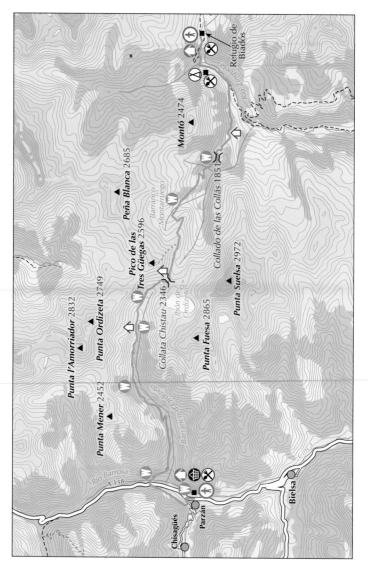

Refugio de Biadós

Montó 2474

Peña Blanca 2685

Barranco Montarruego

Collado de las Collás 1851

Pico de las Tres Güegas 2596

Punta Suelsa 2972

Collata Chistau 2346

Ibón de Ordiceto

Punta Ordizeta 2749

Punta Fuesa 2865

Punta l'Amorriador 2832

Punta Mener 2452

Río Barrosa

A-138

Río Barrosa

Barranco d'Ordiceto

Río Cinca

Bielsa

Chisagüés

Parzán

to continue on top of, or alongside, the buried pipeline. Eventually follow a path which drops down to the road (35min) almost opposite the dirt road heading towards the Ibón de Ordizeto (Lago Urdiceto). ▶ Follow this dirt road across the bridge over the **Río Barrosa** and climb, often high above the **Barranco d'Ordizeto**. Possible dry campsites after another 75min. Pass a spring-fed water-point (2hr 5min), the first water on the climb.

On reaching a 'hydro-electric' sign (2hr 45min) short-cut up a concrete track and then turn left up a path at a 'no entry' sign to regain the track beside a small reservoir. Continue up the track, passing a small bothy (3hr 1980m, N42°40.633 E000°16.416) which was in good condition 2013. If you intend to camp before the col you should do so somewhere near here. Continue up the track until the first switchback (3hr 20min). The GR11 goes straight on along

Some walkers will prefer to just head up the main road and turn right along the dirt road signed 'Lago Urdiceto 11km'.

Río Zinqueta below Refugio de Biadós

Pico de las Tres
Güegas (2596m)
is an easy climb
from here (45min
up, 25min down).

a path where you find your last water until well down the other side of the col. The path rejoins the track just before the **Collata Chistau** (Collata Ordizeto) (3hr 50min, 2346m, N42°40.115 E000°17.318).

The track continues up to the Ibón de Ordizeto, but the GR11 veers left to a small bothy, which was in good condition in 2013, and follows a clear, well-waymarked path, roughly E. The path gains the SE ridge of Pico de las Tres Güegas (4hr 15min). ◄

Descend the grassy ridge until the path veers left (N) at a level spot and descends to the **Barranco Montarruego** (4hr 35min). Water and good campsites. The path veers back E and crosses the stream on a bridge. Continue E or SE through woods to a meadow with a hut, where a track starts. Follow the track, turning left down a rough path immediately after the first switchback, rejoining the track at a stream. Take another shortcut on the left and then follow the track up to the **Collado de las Collás** (5hr 15min, 1851m, N42°39.323 E000°19.972).

Follow the track down, shortcutting a series of switchbacks on paths, and pass a small bothy, Refugio de Lisiert, which was in good condition in 2013 (5hr 30min). Pass left of farm buildings and down to a junction with a dirt road (5hr 50min, 1540m, N42°39.156 E000°21.651). No camping along this road. Turn left up the road, past a youth camp and the Ermita de la Virgin Bianca, to a bar-restaurant and campground at Es Plans.

Camping Forcalla at Es Plans is only open in July and August.

From here head left up a well-waymarked path, which switchbacks the shortcuts in the track, to the **Refugio de Biadós** (6hr 10min, 1760m, N42°39.642 E000°22.642).

Refugio de Biadós is open weekends April–June and fully open mid-June–mid-October.

Facilities on Stage 18
Refugio de Biadós: tel 974 341 613 www.viados.es

STAGE 19

Refugio de Biadós to Puen de San Chaime (Puente de San Jaime)

Start	Refugio de Biadós
Distance	21km; variation GR11-2: Stage 1 11km, Stage 2 17km
Total Ascent	1000m; variation GR11-2: Stage 1 1200m, Stage 2 700m
Total Descent	1500m; variation GR11-2: Stage 1 800m, Stage 2 1600m
Difficulty	The path traverses steep slopes and care will be needed in places. In a high-snow year, snow can linger well into summer on the descent. Stage 1 of the variation GR11-2 takes you over the 2864m Collada Eriste, but the ascent is as easy as you are likely to find on such a high pass. The route is easy to follow in good weather but not recommended for bad weather. The descent on Stage 2 is rough and tough.
Time	6hr 25min; variation GR11-2: Stage 1 5hr 35min, Stage 2 6hr 10min
High Point	Puerto de Chistau (2572m); Collada Eriste (2864m) and Collada de la Plana (2702m) by GR11-2

The GR11 follows a relatively easy route along paths to the Refugio d'Estós over the Puerto de Chistau joining the lovely valleys of Añes Cruces and Estós and then tracks down to Puen de San Chaime. In good weather, it is worth considering taking the longer, tougher but much more spectacular 2-day variation GR11-2, which follows the southern section of the Circuito de los Tres Refugios, which circumnavigates the Posets massif and rejoins the GR11 above Puen de San Chaime.

The GR11 and GR11-2 are used for the **Gran Trail Aneto-Posets**, which circumnavigates the two highest peaks in the Pyrenees, Aneto (3404m) and the Posets (3375m). This 114km trail with 6650m of climb is the route of an annual race held in late July. www.trail-aneto.com

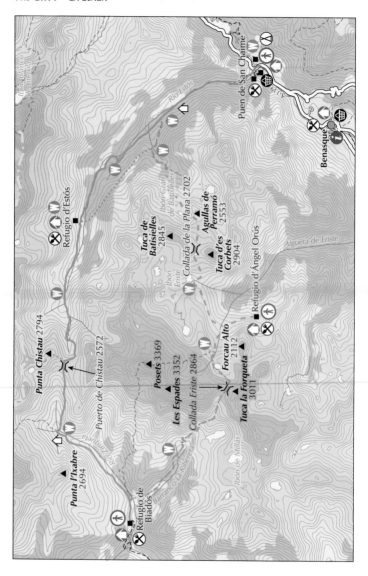

Montó seen over Refugi de Biadós

Follow the track E from the refuge, forking left on a signed path after 10min. This is where the alternative route GR11-2 goes off right. Follow this path to Pleta d'Añes Cruces, the junction of three streams (1hr 30min 2080m). Water and camping. The Cabana d'Añes Cruces on a knoll on the left just before the stream junction is a bothy which was in good condition in 2012. Cross all three streams and follow the path up the valley to the E. The path goes high up the right-hand side of the valley. The only water is likely to be snowmelt streams. Continue to reach the **Puerto de Chistau** (Collau d'Estós) (3hr 5min, 2572m, N42°40.766 E000°26.173). ▶

You could climb Punta Chistau (2794m) by its SW ridge from here (25min up, 15min down).

Veer right and descend easily on a path down scree on the right hand of the valley to cross a stream. Make sure you camp well above the Refugio d'Estós as there is no legal camping on the descent below the refuge. You then cross the **Río Estós** (3hr 55min) before descending the left-hand side, high above the stream by the time you reach the **Refugio d'Estós** (4hr 35min, 1890m, N42°40.527 E000°29.123). The refuge is not visible from above and only comes into view when you are very near.

Refugio d'Estós, a popular manned refuge with full facilities, is open all year.

133

Río Estós

Continue down the left-hand side of the valley, crossing to the right-hand side at a bridge and past a hut, Cabaña d'el Tormio. Follow the dirt road which starts from this hut. After a few minutes there is a sign indicating the GR11 forking

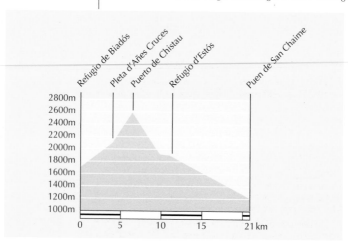

left and dropping down to a poor viewpoint of the cascades in the Río Estós before regaining the road. There seems little point in taking this diversion and you are better to follow the road. Pass the junction where alternate route rejoins the GR11 (5hr 40min) and soon pass a spring with piped water. Continue past the Refugio de Santa Ana (5hr 50min). This small bothy was in good condition in 2013.

Continue down the road to a large car park. Follow the tarmac road, ignoring a turn going right to the Hostal Parque Natural, and turn right at the bottom of the hill to cross the bridge over the Río Esera at **Puen de San Chaime** (6hr 25min, 1250m). Camping Aneto is on the right and Camping Ixeia is 5min along the route for Stage 20.

> Puen de San Chaime has a hostal and two camp-grounds: Camping Aneto has bar-restaurant, super-market, cabins and bunkhouse accommodation and the shop stocks 'original' and 'easy-clic' camping gas, Camping Ixeia has bar-restaurant, cabins and bunkhouse.
>
> The tourist resort of Benasque is 3km to the SW and has all services, including a mountain equip-ment shop which stocks all types of camping gas. There are buses in summer from Benasque to Puen de San Chaime continuing up the dirt road all the way to the Refugio del Puen de Corones.

Variation GR11-2

Stage 1 Refugio de Biadós to Refugio d'Ángel Orús

Follow the GR11 for about 12min then fork right (signed) and cross the **Río Zinqueta** and follow the path through delightful wood and meadow high above the left bank of the Barranco la Ribereta. After crossing the Barranco las Tuertas (1hr 25min) the gradient steepens. The last camping before the col is as you reach the treeline. Eventually reach a signpost (2hr, N42°38.500 E000°24.795) where the 'tourist' path veers right to Ibón de Millás. The GR11-2 heads steeply uphill on a faint path. The gradient eases (2hr 50min) and climbs ESE up the long valley to the obvious col, **Collada Eriste** (3hr 50min, 2864m, N42°38.023 E000°25.656).

Head down E, veering NE, to go left of Ibón Llardaneta and continue down the well-marked path. The first good

Ibón Llardaneta

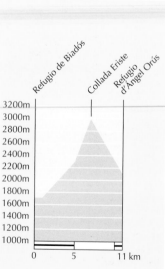

camping on the descent is on the left at about 2460m. You soon cross a bridge over the Barranco Llardaneta and descend to a junction with a signpost (5hr 5min, 2370m, N42°38.036 E000°27.061). If you don't need the refuge you can turn left here and start Stage 2. Otherwise veer right and descend to **Refugio d'Ángel Orús** (5hr 35min, 2112m, N42°37.650 E000°27.455), situated at the foot of the E ridge of Forcau Alto (2865m).

> You could climb **Posets** (3369m), one of the easiest 3000m peaks, from the refuge. The path goes off left as you descend from Ibón Llardaneta.
>
> Refugio d'Ángel Orús is a manned refuge with full refuge facilities.

Stage 2 Refugio d'Ángel Orús to Puen de San Chaime

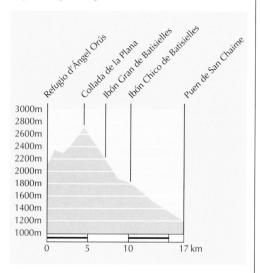

Return to the signed junction at 2370m (45min) and fork right. Cross the Barranco Llardaneta and traverse to the Cabana de Llardana which was roofless in 2013. ▸ The path gradually climbs and veers left to reach the outlet stream from Ibón Eriste (1hr 45min, 2394m, N42°38.600 E000°27.907). Last camping before the col. Cross and veer right before climbing easily ENE to arrive at the Ibón de la Plana. The path goes above the left bank and up to the obvious **Collada de la Plana** (2hr 55min, 2702m, N42°38.532 E000°28.647). Good legal campsites are in short supply on the descent.

Follow the path, or footprints in the snow, easily aiming to the left of the Agullas de Perramó (2553m), the peak to the E which splits the valley in descent. At the foot of this peak the route heads steeply down (N) and care is needed to follow the cairns and waymarks (mainly blue dots). The gradient eases, but the terrain remains rough, as you pass to the right of three small lakes and descend to the **Ibón Gran de Batisielles** (4hr 15min, 2209m, N42°39.070 E000°29.963). The path now improves as it descends to the tiny Ibón

The faint path is cairned with occasional waymarks and could be difficult to follow in bad weather.

Chico de Batisielles (4hr 45min, 1861m, N42°39.253 E000°30.601) where there is a bothy that you could use if you were desperate.

There is now a choice of routes to rejoin the GR11. You could continue along the GR11-2, forking left, to reach the Refugio d'Estós in about 90min. The more direct route, recommended here, forks right and follows the 'tourist' path, signed to Cabana de Santa Ana. Reach the good descent track (5hr 25min, 1552m, N42°39.167 E000°31.562) from the Refugio d'Estós and turn right along the GR11 to **Puen de San Chaime** as described under Stage 19 (6hr 10min).

Facilities on Stage 19
Refugio d'Estós: tel 974 344 515 www.refugiodeestos.com
Hostal Parque Natural and bar-restaurant: tel 974 344 584
    www.hostalparquenatural.com
Camping Aneto: tel 974 551 141 www.campinganeto.com
Camping Ixeia: tel 974 552 129 www.campingixeia.es
Benasque Oficina de Turismo : tel 974 551 289 www.turismobenasque.com
Refugio d'Ángel Orús: tel 974 344 044 www.refugioangelorus.com

STAGE 20

Puen de San Chaime to Refugio de Cap de Llauset

Start	Puen de San Chaime
Distance	18km
Total Ascent	1700m
Total Descent	400m
Difficulty	This is a rough, tough stage with much boulderfield but fortunately the waymarking is excellent. Snow can linger over the pass well into summer.
Time	6hr 20min
High Point	Collado de Ballibierna (2732m)
Note	At the time of writing the only accommodation between Puen de San Chaime and the Refugi de Conangles (at the end of Stage 21) are three bothies, all in excellent condition in 2013. The foundations of a new 80-bed refuge, Refugio de Cap de Llauset, were laid in 2012. It is hoped that construction will be completed in 2015. Until the new refuge is opened the only option for those not equipped for camping or using unmanned refuges is to combine Stages 20 and 21, with a walking time of about 10hr. This could be reduced if you caught the early morning bus from Benasque or Puen de San Jaime to the Puen del Corones, saving almost 3hr.

This stage starts with a long walk up a dirt road. Fortunately, the only traffic on this closed road is likely to be the minibus which operates from Benasque to Puen del Corones. There follows the crossing of one of the toughest passes on the GR11.

The GR11 turns left along a dirt road, passing a track to Camping Ixeia. Shortcut left just after the first switchback then turn left along the along the E shore of the **Embalse de Paso Nuebo** to reach a major junction (45min). Turn right up the concrete road. There is frequent water on the climb ahead. 10min later the GR11 takes a steep shortcut to the right, but you might prefer to stay on the dirt road for a steady climb. Turn right on regaining the road as it climbs steadily

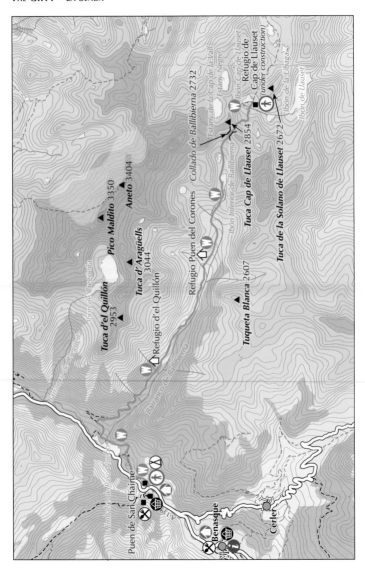

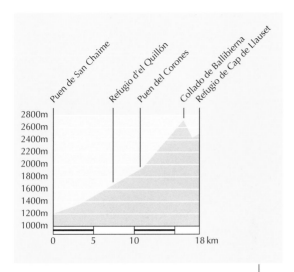

up a gorge lined with granite cliffs. Pass the **Refugio d'el Quillón**, just above you on the left (2hr). This small bothy was in excellent condition in 2013. Continue to the roadhead at the Puen del Corones (2hr 40min, 1980m, N42°36.623 E000°37.262). The **Refugio Puen del Corones** is a large bothy and was in excellent condition in 2013. Camping is not allowed in the vicinity of the bothy, but there are plenty of good campsites further up the valley.

Follow the well-waymarked track roughly E from the refuge. The track becomes a path before you reach a flat area, Pleta de Llosas (3hr 35min). Turn right, signed to Ibones de Ballibierna, cross a bridge and climb a sparsely wooded ridge to cross the outlet of the **Ibón Inferior de Ballibierna**, which is followed to the lake (4hr 20min, 2440m). The route from here is complex as well as being rough and tough with boulderfields and crags. Continue along the N shore of the lower lake and up the ridge to the E to reach the Ibón Superior de Ballibierna (4hr 55min). Camping is possible at this corrie lake. Continue up a combination of path, boulderfield and possibly snowfield to reach the **Collado de Ballibierna** (5hr 40min 2732m, N42°36.169 E000°40.497).

Ibón de Ballibierna from Collada de Ballibierna

A GR11 variant via the Ibón de Llauset goes right from here.

The descent is slightly easier, but there are still boulderfields. Fortunately the complex route is well waymarked. Turn left at a signpost (6hr) and down to another signpost by a stream (6hr 15min, 2410m).

◄ The GR11 continues left from here, as described under Stage 21. Once construction is complete, you will probably want to visit the **Refugio de Cap de Llauset** which has been visible on the descent (6hr 20min, 2450m, N42°35.747 E000°41.050).

Facilities on Stage 20
Once open, details of the new Refugio de Cap de Llauset should be found at www.fames.com.

STAGE 21

Refugio de Cap de Llauset to Refugi de Conangles

Start	Refugio de Cap de Llauset
Distance	11km
Total Ascent	200m
Total Descent	1100m
Difficulty	Although mainly downhill this is a tough section with boulderfield to cross and a steep descent.
Time	3hr 30min
High Point	Collada d'es Ibons (2524m)
Note	See note in the introduction to Stage 20 about the Refugio de Cap de Llauset. This stage used to end at the Espitau de Vielha (Hospital de Viella) but this refuge no longer offers accommodation. Expect new waymarking and minor rerouting when the Refugio de Cap de Llauset opens.

The magnificent scenery continues on the long, tough descent to the Refugi de Conangles.

From the signpost at the end of Stage 20 head upstream, veering right to the Ibón Cap de Llauset (15min). Excellent campsites on the NW shore. Follow the path round the S shore and head SE to the **Collada d'es Ibons** (35min, 2524m, N42°35.579 E000°41.379). Descend down boulderfield to the three Estanys Cap d'Angliós and along the S shore, mainly on boulderfield. It would be possible to camp by these lakes, but there are better sites ahead by the Estany de Baix, after which camping opportunities in the descent are very limited. Continue down grassy slopes to a sign just below the **Refugio d'Angliós** (1hr 20min, 2220m, N42°35.409 E000°42.567). This small bothy, which is a little left of the waymarked path, was in excellent condition in 2013. ▶

The path continues down to and along the S shore of the **Estany de Baix**, before descending a well-waymarked rough path high above the right-hand bank of the Barranco d'Angliós. A steep descent leads to a path junction, with

An alternative route of the GR11 from the Ibón de Llauset rejoins the main route here.

Refugio d'Angliós

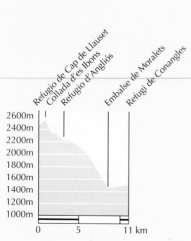

Refugio de Cap de Llauset
Collada d'es Ibons
Refugio d'Angliós
Embalse de Moralets
Refugi de Conangles

2600m
2400m
2200m
2000m
1800m
1600m
1400m
1200m
1000m

0   5   11 km

signpost and picnic table, beside
the **Ríu Ixalenques** (2hr 30min).
Turn right along an easier path
for a pleasant descent of the
right-hand side of the river. At
the bottom, steps lead right to the
main road (**N-230**) (3hr, 1460m)
at the N end of the **Embalse de
Moralets**.

Turn left across the road
bridge and follow the road until
there is a track on the right. Take
the track, immediately crossing
a bridge and turning left. A waymarked combination of track,
path and river bed leads through
wood and meadow along the Ríu
Ribagorzana. At the **Barranc de
Besiberri** you need to head a little upstream to cross the bridge

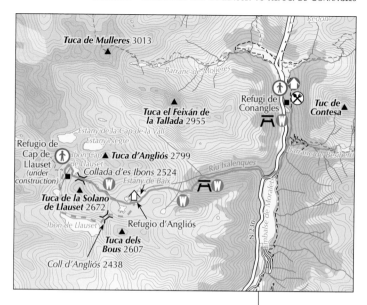

before descending again to the river. Continue until you pass a picnic area with large car park, on your left. Keep going up a tarmac track and soon reach the **Refugi de Conangles**, on your left (3hr 30min, 1555m, N42°36.894 E000°46.115).

Refugi de Conangles, with full refuge facilities, is open all year.

Facilities on Stage 21
Refugi de Conangles: tel 619 847 077 www.refugiconangles.com

STAGE 22
Refugi de Conangles to Refugi dera Restanca

Start	Refugi de Conangles
Distance	13km
Total Ascent	1100m
Total Descent	600m
Difficulty	The majority of this section is on good mountain paths with only a little difficult terrain. The route is cairned with only occasional waymarks.
Time	5hr
High Point	Pòrt de Rius (2355m)

The route passes through magnificent granite scenery. If the weather is good and you have time to spare it is worth following the alternative route via Lac de Mer.

Return to the track and continue until you cross the Barranc de Lac Redon (15min) with signpost. Turn right up the left-hand side of the stream to another signpost at a path junction (25min). The path left takes you to the Espitau de Vielha,

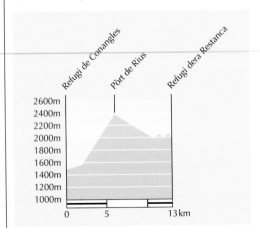

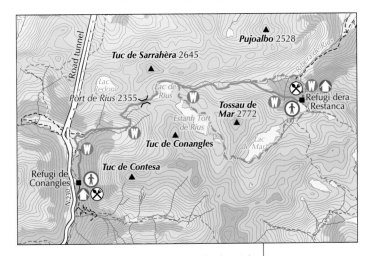

which is no longer a refuge. The GR11 turns right, then right again along a track (40min). Turn left off the track just before a bridge and cross the Barranc de Lac Redon. Follow a well-cairned path with occasional waymarks. There are camping opportunities and water early on this ascent. As you climb the path veers left (N then W) before reaching a path junction (1hr 45min). The left path goes to Lac Redon but the GR11 switchbacks sharp right (NE) and climbs easily up to the **Pòrt de Rius** (2hr 30min, 2355m, N42°38.127 E000°47.507). The path now stays fairly level as it traverses above a pond and then along the N shore of **Lac de Rius**. Camping possible, but better sites just ahead. Cross the often dry outlet stream at the E end of the lake (3hr 5min).

> The Haute Randonnée Pyrénénne goes off right here to the Estanh Tòrt de Rius and the Lac de Mar to rejoin the GR11 at the Refugi dera Restanca. It takes about 4hr to reach the Refugi dera Restanca from the Lac de Rius by this magnificent alternative to the GR11.

Follow the path down the right bank of the often dry **Ribèra de Rius**. After about 8min you pass a crag on your right out of which a little spring flows from a small pipe.

*Scouts above
Hospital de Viella*

Just below the spring is a flat area with excellent campsites (3hr 30min). Continue easily down the right-hand side of the valley until the path forks (4hr, 1943m, N42°38.445 E000°51.267).

If you don't intend to visit the Refugi dera Restanca, but are intending to take the official (northern) route of the GR11 on Stage 23, you could **shortcut** by forking left from here to rejoin the GR11 at the Cabana de Rius.

If you require the Refugi dera Restanca, or if you are taking the highly recommended GR11-18 variation on Stage 23, you should fork right here. The path now becomes rougher as it climbs over a ridge (4hr 20min) and descends to a stream. It then climbs a second ridge, under a power-line. Follow the waymarks and cairns carefully, as it would be easy to lose the route. From the ridge it is just a few minutes descent to the **Refugi dera Restanca** (5hr, 2010m, N42°38.085 E000°51.267) at the E end of the dam. Camping is not allowed in the vicinity of the refuge.

Refugi dera Restanca, a manned refuge with full refuge facilities, is open roughly June to late September. Central booking operates for this and other refuges in the area.

The Refugi dera Restanca is one of the refuges on the popular **Carros de Foc** (chariots of fire) tour in the Parque Nacional de Aigüestortes i Estany de Sant Maurici, which is a tour of nine manned refuges in the Park: Amitges, Saboredo, Colomèrs, Restanca, Ventosa i Calvell, Estany Llong, Colomina, Josep Maria Blanc and Ernest Mallafré. For those with a competitive urge, the Carros de Foc Sky Runner takes place at the beginning of September, when the challenge is to complete the route in 24 hours. www.carrosdefoc.com

Facilities on Stage 22
Refugi dera Restanca: www.restanca.com. Central reservations: tel 973 641 681 www.refusonline.com

Refugi dera Restanca, Estany dera Restanca

STAGE 23
*Refugi dera Restanca to Refugi de Colomèrs
(by Port de Caldes, GR11-18)*

Start	Refugi dera Restanca
Distance	8km; official GR11: 13km
Total Ascent	700m; official GR11: 1100m
Total Descent	600m; official GR11: 900m
Difficulty	There are quite a lot of boulderfields to cross and care will be needed with navigation in bad weather. The official GR11 is relatively easy with much of the route being along tracks.
Time	3hr 30min; official GR11: 5hr 5min
High Point	Coret d'Oelhacrestada (2475m), Pòrt de Caldes (2570m)

It is strongly recommended that you follow the superb southerly variant route, the GR11-18, described here, rather than the official GR11. The GR11-18 used to be the official route of the GR11, but it has been replaced by the northerly route, which follows tracks much of the way. There is no technical difficulty with the southern route. This short day passes through a landscape of countless tarns in magnificent granite scenery. There would be plenty of time to climb the popular Montardo (2833m).

The path along the shoreline is the route taken by the HRP in descending from the Lac de Mar. The GR11-18 follows the higher path, roughly SE, which climbs to Lac deth Cap de Pòrt (35min, 2230m). Head along the N shore of this beautiful lake and up well-waymarked boulderfield to the **Coret d'Oelhacrestada** (1hr 30min, 2475m, N42°37.575 E000°52.528). There is a confusion of footpaths here. Stick with the inadequately waymarked 'main' path which climbs to an unnamed col (1hr 45min, 2520m, N42°37.510 E000°52.937) to the ESE.

At the low point between these two cols several cairned paths head up towards the SE ridge of **Montardo**. They join higher up and when you reach

Summit of Montardo

the ridge follow the good path left to the summit of Montardo (45min up, 30min down).

From the unnamed col, paths are well cairned with occasional way-marks and are easy to follow. The obvious col ahead (roughly ESE) is the Pòrt de Caldes, but first you must descend to the S end of the Estany del Pòrt de Caldes (2hr) before climbing easily to the **Pòrt de Caldes** (2hr 30min, 2570m, N42°37.298 E000°53.740). The path now descends roughly E to reach a stream. Descend the left-hand side of this stream until just above **Lac Major de Colomèrs**. Turn right, at a sign, to the large modern **Refugi de Colomèrs** (3hr 30min, 2135m, N42°37.455 E000°55.253) on the W shore of the

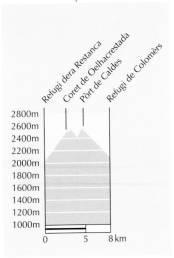

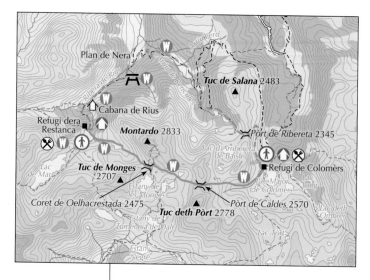

reservoir. The old refuge on the W end of the dam is now closed and locked.

Refugi de Colomèrs, a manned refuge with full refuge facilities, is fully open June to late September. See website for opening outside of this period. Central booking operates for this refuge.

The official GR11 is longer and less scenic than the recommended GR11-18 variation.

Official GR11 by the Pòrt de Ribereta

◀ Return across the dam and turn right down a good path to reach a track at **Cabana de Rius** (40min). This bothy was in good condition in 2013. Turn right and continue descending, passing a track on the left to a picnic site beside the river. Shortly afterwards reach another junction (1hr 5min, 1420m) and turn right, signed to Montcasau (no GR waymarks). Follow a good track which switchbacks up the hillside, eventually to reach a junction (2hr 15min). Turn sharp right, signed to Montcasau, and when this track ends (2hr 35min) head up a steep path to the left of the outlet stream from the Estany de Montcasau. Probably your last water until just before the end of the section.

Dam at Refugi de Restanca

Reach the dam (3hr 5min) and follow a good path above the left-hand side of the two lakes. This path switchbacks easily up the steep slopes to the **Pòrt de Ribereta** (4hr 5min, 2345m, N42°38.109 E000°54.835).

The descent starts to the left before switchbacking down the steep slope an turning right (S) on a rising traverse to an unnamed col above **Lac Major de Colomèrs** (4hr 55min, 2207m, N42°37.608 E000°55.110). Descend to a junction with the GR11-18 and turn left, then right, to the **Refugi de Colomèrs** (5hr 5min).

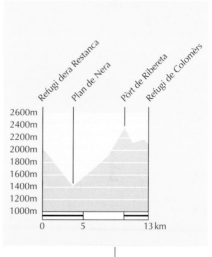

Facilities on Stage 23
Refugi de Colomèrs: tel 973 253 008 www.refugicolomers.com. Central reservations: tel 973 641 681 www.refusonline.com

STAGE 24
Refugi de Colomèrs to Espot

Start	Refugi de Colomèrs
Distance	18km
Total Ascent	500m
Total Descent	1300m
Difficulty	A relatively easy section, but navigation could be tricky in bad weather
Time	5hr 50min
High Point	Pòrt de Ratèra (2590m)

This is a magnificent walk through the Parque Nacional de Aigüestortes i Estany de Sant Maurici. The area around the Estany de Sant Maurici is understandably popular with tourists and the tourist path offers a pleasant descent down to Espot. It is worth considering balancing Stages 24 and 25 better by ending this section at the Refugi d'Amitges, which is a little off route, or at Refugi Ernest Mallafré close to the Estany de Sant Maurici and then going straight through to La Guingueta d'Àneu on the next day. This would leave plenty of time to climb Tuc de Ratèra (2857m).

From the new refuge, take the path to the old refuge on the W end of the dam and cross the dam. Descend a little at the end of the dam then veer right (E) and climb to a pass, **Coret de Clòto** (30min). There are plenty of good campsites and water all the way up to the Pòrt de Ratèra. The Pòrt de Ratèra is the obvious col to the SE. From here you head slightly right, contouring roughly SE, ignoring sideturns, to reach **Lac Long**.

Follow the path along the SW shore of Lac Long and Lac Redon to reach **Lac Obago** (1hr 5min). On the left, just before reaching this lake, you will see a bothy, Refugi Lac Obago, unfortunately roofless in 2013. Ignore old waymarks which fork right away from the lake and follow the path round the lake until you are SE of it, then head SE up the path to the **Pòrt de Ratèra**. This broad grassy pass has a false col, then a slight drop with a path (GR211-4) going off left to the Refugi de Saboredo before the highpoint (2hr 25min, 2590m, N42°36.235 E000°57.495).

Tuc de Ratèra to the right of the col is an easy climb. Follow the cairned path which climbs the E face of Tuc de Ratèra and when the path reaches the

Lac Long

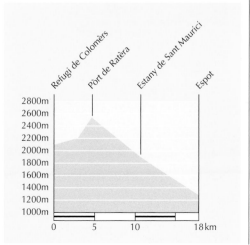

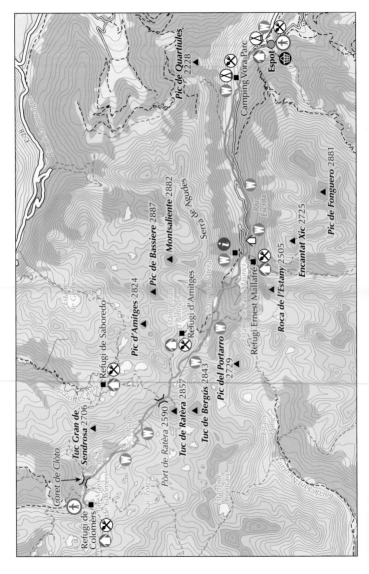

rocky summit ridge, turn left to the summit (40min up, 25min down).

The descent is marked by wooden posts with GR markings. Follow the path, initially contouring E, ignoring any sideturns, including a left fork to the Refugi d'Amitges.

Refugi d'Amitges is a popular manned refuge with full refuge facilities.

Continue to descend, mainly SE, to the upper waters of the Ríu de Ratèra and follow the stream down, crossing it four times before reaching a junction (3hr 20min). Fork right and pass left of the Estanyols de Crabes before crossing the stream again and reaching a dirt road (3hr 40min). Turn left, ignore a sharp left turn to the Refugi d'Amitges and pass along the S shore of the **Estany de Ratèra**. Cross a bridge across the Ríu de Ratèra and immediately turn right down a path.

Soon turn right at a path junction and descend past a big waterfall, which attracts the tourists, to reach the **Estany de Sant Maurici**. There is a National Park Information Office, water-point and toilets at the E end of this reservoir (4hr 20min, 1920m, N42°34.858 E001°00.661).

Estany de Sant Maurici

Turn right along a track beneath the dam, past the toilets, soon veering E. After a few minutes a track goes off right to Refugi Ernest Mallafré.

Refugi Ernest Mallafré is a manned refuge with full refuge facilities.

Pass the Capella de Sant Maurici (4hr 30min) which has a water-point, a shady seating area and a small bothy which was in good condition 2013. Soon after the chapel, fork right down an excellent 'tourist' path. Keep straight on across a tarmac road as you continue down the left-hand side of the Ríu Escrita. Fork left (5hr) along a grassy track when the tourists fork right to their car park. After a right fork you leave the National Park and the track becomes a good path which you follow until it eventually crosses the Ríu Escrita on a bridge (5hr 30min). Turn left down the road, passing a dirt road to **Camping Vora Parc**. As you enter **Espot**, stay immediately right of the river. Camping Solau is across the river. Continue down to reach the centre of Espot (5hr 50min, 1330m, N42°34.546 E001°0.292).

Espot is a tourist village with a good selection of hotels, Casa Rural, campgrounds, shops, bars and restaurants (some listed below). The small outdoor store stocks 'easy-clic' camping gas. Land Rover taxis take tourists from Espot to Estany de Sant Maurici and Estany d'Amitges. **www.taxisespot.com**

Facilities on Stage 24

Refugi d'Amitges: tel 973 250 109 www.amitges.com Central reservations: tel 973 641 681 www.refusonline.com

Refugi Ernest Mallafré: tel 973 250 118. Central reservations: tel 93 372 02 83 http://feec.cat

Hotel Roca Blanca: tel 973 624 156 www.rocablanca.net

Els Encantats Hotel: tel 973 624 138 http://hotelencantats.com

Hotel Roya: tel 973 624 040 www.hotelroya.net

Hotel Saurat: tel 973 624 162 www.hotelsaurat.com

Camping Vora Parc has bar-restaurant, minimarket and 'luxury' tents. Tel 973 624 108 www.voraparc.com

Camping Solau also operates two Casa Rural with reasonably priced rooms: tel 973 624 068 www.camping-solau.com

STAGE 25

Espot to La Guingueta d'Àneu

Start	Espot
Distance	10km
Total Ascent	200m
Total Descent	600m
Difficulty	Easy
Time	2hr 25min
High Point	Estaís (1400m)

This is not much more than a 'rest day'. The next few days are in the foothills of the Pyrenees and there is a break from alpine terrain until the crossing into Andorra. Water can be difficult to find in these dry hills.

Leave Espot down the street immediately right of the river. The route is well signed and soon becomes a good track. After 15min pass a covered seating area and shortly afterwards fork left down a path then turn sharp left down a rough track. Cross the stream at the bottom and climb to the main road (35min, 1250m). **Camping La Mola** is on your left.

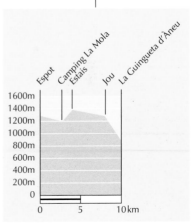

> Camping La Mola also has bar-restaurant, supermarket and cabins.

Cross the road and follow the path opposite. This path shortcuts the switchbacks on the road to Jou. As you cross a ridge turn left up a track which leads to **Estaís** (1hr, 1400m). The waymarks going left from the church square take you on a tour of the hamlet before exiting E from the N corner along a tarmac

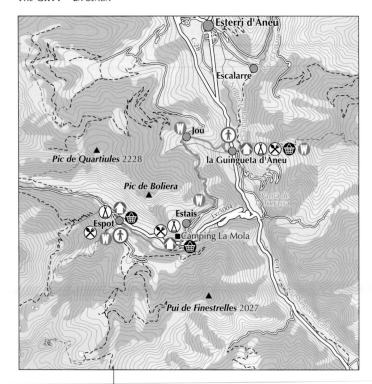

road. You soon fork left along an old path which contours,
rounding the ridge and then gradually descends to meet the
road to Jou (1hr 25min).

Turn left, soon passing piped water from a woodland
stream and continue along the road to **Jou** (1hr 55min,
1320m). If you want water, fork left into Jou and pass two
water-points. Otherwise continue along the 'main' road and,
at the last house, fork right down steps then fork right down
a path. At a viewpoint near the bottom of the hill veer right
onto a track which soon becomes a tarmac road. Turn left at
a junction down to **La Guingueta d'Àneu** (2hr 25min, 950m,
N42°35.612 E001°07.918). The water-point, and seating
area, is a little S of the Poldo Hotel.

The hamlet of Jou

La Guingueta d'Àneu is a hamlet with hotel, hostal and two campgrounds. Nou Camping also has cabins, bar-restaurant and small supermarket which stocks 'original' and 'easy-clic' camping gas. There are buses to Lleida and Barcelona.

Facilities on Stage 25
Camping La Mola: tel 973 624 024 www.campinglamola.com
Hotel Poldo: tel 973 626 080 www.hotelpoldo.com
Hostal Orteu: tel 973 626 086
Nou Camping: tel 973 626 261 www.noucamping.com
Camping Vall d'Àneu: tel 973 626 390

STAGE 26
La Guingueta d'Àneu to Estaon

Start	La Guingueta d'Àneu
Distance	10km
Total Ascent	1400m
Total Descent	1100m
Difficulty	Although a fairly short day it is tough because of the steepness of both ascent and descent. There is inadequate waymarking on the ascent from Dorve.
Time	5hr 10min
High Point	Coll de Montcaubo (2201m)

It is worth making an early start on this stage as the long steep ascent could be very tiring in the full heat of the day. It is also worth carrying plenty of water from Dorve. This is the stage on the GR11 where you are most likely to lose the route so pay careful attention to your navigation.

Follow the road to Dorve from the seating area to the S of the Poldo Hotel. Cross the bridge, turn right along the lake.

Seventeen **machine gun nests** were built around La Guingueta as part of Franco's Pyrenean defence line but curiously these defences were constructed between 1947 and 1952, well after the end of the Spanish Civil War or World War II. There is a well-preserved example on your left as you walk alongside the lake.

Fork left up the new road to Dorve. It would be possible to walk up this quiet road but the GR11 soon forks left up the old path to Dorve which shortcuts the switchbacks on the road. The path is signed at road crossings and cairned with occasional waymarks. It leads straight into hamlet of **Dorve** (1hr 15min, 1390m). Dorve just missed out on the building boom and most of the houses are still derelict. Water-point. The next water will probably be just before you reach Estaon.

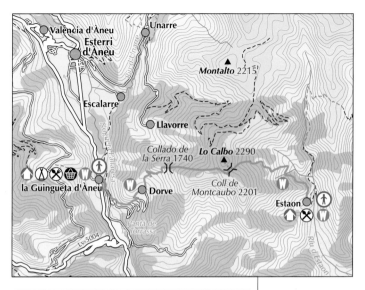

Machine gun bunker beside the lake

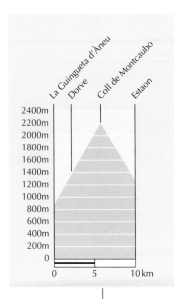

Lo Calbo (2290m), with its communication masts, is easily climbed from here (10min up, 5 min down).

Go round the right-hand side of the church, after which the path veers back left.

The next section is inadequately waymarked and it is easy to lose the path. The pass you are aiming for is much higher up the ridge than the more obvious pass over which the path to Llavorre goes. As soon as you are clear of the woods get out your compass and check which part of the ridge is NE of Dorve. This is the location of the pass you are aiming for. It is easy to get too far left on the ascent up vague switchbacks. About 10min after leaving Dorve fork left. The vague path approaches the ridge N of Dorve, and then veers E before resuming the switchbacking climb to the **Collado de la Serra** on the ridge (2hr 20min, 1740m, N42°35.834 E001°09.355).

From the pass turn right (E) along a clear path which could be rough unless there is regular maintenance to prevent trees encroaching on the trail. The path takes you through the forest to a meadow (3hr 15min). Dry campsites. Continue through the meadow and back into the forest, turning left at a path junction (3hr 15min) and continuing up to the ridge (3hr 30min, 2110m). Turn left up the ridge, but soon fork right and leave the ridge to traverse the SW slopes of Calbo to reach its SE ridge. Take care here, ignoring a path which continues along the ridge. The route, marked by cairns, swings left to reach the **Coll de Montcaubo** (3hr 45min, 2201m, N42°35.728 E001°10.852). Good dry campsites. ◀

The path descends steeply NE from the col, gradually veering E, then SE. The route is fairly easy to follow despite the waymarks being in need of repainting (2013). Turn left at an old telegraph pole (4hr 20min) and right (S) at a junction (4hr 40min). This path soon crosses a woodland stream, the first reliable water since Dorve, although you may want to treat it before drinking. An ancient path now drops gently down to **Estaon**. Follow the 'main' street down to the water-point and refuge in the centre of the hamlet (5hr 10min, 1240m, N42°35.282 E001°12.618).

Refugi d'Estaon is open from about 24 June to 15 September and can be opened at weekends outside this period with a telephone reservation. Casa Motxo also offers accommodation in Estaon.

Facilities on Stage 26
Refugi d'Estaon: tel 625 274 259 http://refugiestaon.com
Casa Motxo: tel 973 623 123

STAGE 27

Estaon to Tavascan

Start	Estaon
Distance	12km
Total Ascent	1000m
Total Descent	1200m
Difficulty	Easy
Time	3hr 50min
High Point	Coll de Jou (1830m)

This is an easy day through an area which would have been a thriving agricultural area in the past, but is now largely deserted.

Continue down the street to the end of Estaon and turn left along an old path which gradually drops down to the **Ríu d'Estaon**. Cross it on a bridge (10min) to reach a dirt road and turn left. Follow the road as it crosses the river, turn right (25min) across a bridge and follow the old path up the right-hand bank of the river. Rejoin the road when it again crosses the river. A Parc Natural sign reminds you that camping is not allowed except between 20:00 and 8:00. After 40min the dirt road ends and an old path continues up the right-hand side of the stream to **Bordes de Nibros** (1hr 5min, 1480m). This deserted hamlet is largely derelict.

Deserted hamlet of Bordes de Nibros

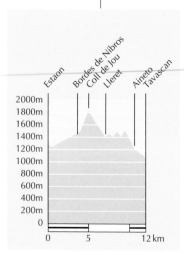

Your next water is likely to be at Lleret. Continue up the stream then turn sharp right at a signed junction (1hr 15min). Pass a barn and switchback up the hill, going left of another barn, to reach the **Coll de Jou** (2hr 5min, 1830m N42°36.872 E001°13.221). Dry camping is possible at the col or at several places on the descent. Follow the path down from the col to a cattle trough then follow a poor track, initially SE, which switchbacks down to a bigger track. Turn left at this junction (2hr 25min) and contour before switchbacking down to Lleret. The water-point with a seating area is at the top of the hamlet.

Continue down the tarmac access road to the first switchback and turn left up an old path. Soon cross a stream and shortly afterwards fork left and cross another stream before making a spectacular high-level traverse. Eventually this good path ends and you descend steeply down a well-waymarked path to **Aineto** (3hr 35min, 1220m).

Water-point on your left. Continue up a concrete ramp between the houses, keep straight on to the end of the hamlet and then turn left down another old path which takes you to **Tavascan**. Keep straight on past a water-point and over the ancient bridge, then turn right to the information office on the main road (3hr 50min, 1120m). All the tourist facilities in Tavascan are to your right.

> Tavascan has good facilities for tourists for such a small village, including a small food shop.
> Casa Feliu has a bar-restaurant and accommodation. Hotel Llacs de Cardos offers an early breakfast and discounts to GR11 hikers. Hotel Estanys Blaus is the up-market part of the Llacs de Cardos organisation with the same contact details. The hotel owns the small outdoor store opposite the hotel, which sells 'easy-clic' and 'Coleman-style' camping gas. If the food shop or the outdoor store

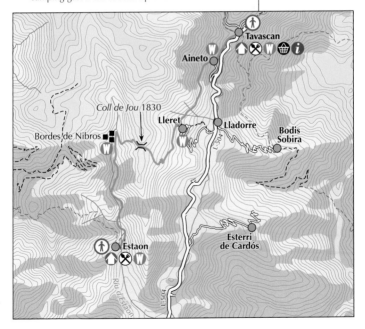

is closed when you are passing through ask at the Llacs de Cardos hotel and they will find someone to open them for you!

Facilities on Stage 27
Casa Feliu: tel 973 623 163
Hotel Llacs de Cardos: tel 973 623 179 www.llacscardos.com
Marxant Hotel: tel 973 623 151 www.hotelmarxant.com
Tavascan Information Office: tel 973 623 089

STAGE 28
Tavascan to Àreu

Start	Tavascan
Distance	16km
Total Ascent	1800m
Total Descent	1600m
Difficulty	Easy
Time	6hr 10min
High Point	Coll de Tudela (2243m)

This is a final easy section in the foothills before returning to the alpine mountains.

Cross the bridge by the information office and follow a path which climbs steeply until you come to a signpost by some ruined stone huts (1hr 15min, 1530m). Keep straight on and contour along an old path, crossing four woodland streams before reaching **Boldis Subira** (2hr 20min, 1510m, N42°36.810 E001°16.350). Care is needed as the exposed path is crumbling in places. There are several water points in Boldis Subira, but the one on the right as you exit the hamlet is probably the best quality.

Keep going in the same direction and leave along a signed track, which veers E to cross a pair of streams before veering SW. The track switchbacks left when it reaches the Roc Bataller ridge (3hr 5min) and right (3hr 40min) to

Bridge at Tavascan

return to the ridge. Head up the ridge through brush and almost immediately turn left and then right along a grassy 'ride'. Dry camping is possible here. This 'ride' climbs the

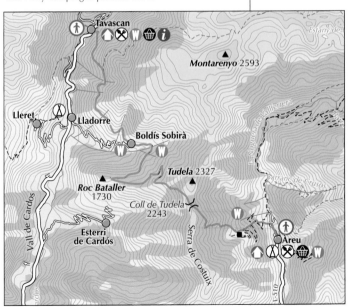

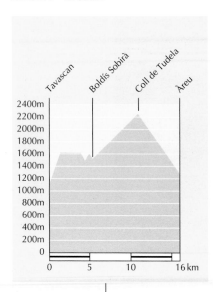

ridge and becomes a clear path by the time it crosses the now grassy track by a signpost, then climbs through brush and forest on the SW slopes of Tudela to reach the grassy S ridge with a signpost and corral. Veer left across the **Coll de Tudela** (4hr 50min, 2243m, N42°35.837 E001°17.663). Dry camping. Follow a clear path, initially SE, as it switchbacks down to Boredes de Costuix in meadows (5hr 30min). Camping possible. Descend between buildings, continue down and after about 30m you will see a track on your right, which you follow past a water-point in a gully. Immediately afterwards the GR11 forks left down a path. This path shortcuts many switchbacks on the track and can be followed all the way down to the road at the N end of **Àreu** (6hr 5min). Water-point on the right at the junction. If you don't want Àreu you can turn left here and start Stage 29. Otherwise turn right to the centre of Àreu (6hr 10min).

Àreu has a small shop, hotel, and several Casa Rural offering accommodation. The shop stocks 'original' camping gas. Camping Pica d'Estats, which also has bar-restaurant and cabins, is open April–October.

Facilities on Stage 28
Hotel Vallferrera: tel 973 624 343 www.hotelvallferrera.com
Casa Besolí: tel 973 624 415
Camping Pica d'Estats: tel 973 624 347 www.picadestats.com

STAGE 29

Àreu to Refugi de Vallferrera

Start	Àreu
Distance	9km
Total Ascent	900m
Total Descent	200m
Difficulty	Easy
Time	3hr 15min
High Point	Refugi de Vallferrera (1920m)

This short walk up the Vall Ferrera is popular with the tourists. It sets you up for the high-level crossing into Andorra the next day. If you are camping or are happy to use an unmanned refuge you will probably want to continue further up the valley.

Head up the road that soon becomes a dirt road, which may be busy with tourist cars. Fork right across the **Ríu Noguera de Vallferrera** (45min) and 5min later fork right up an old path which climbs steadily. When you reach a meadow with some barns (1hr 30min), the path goes between walls to the

Refugi de Vallferrera

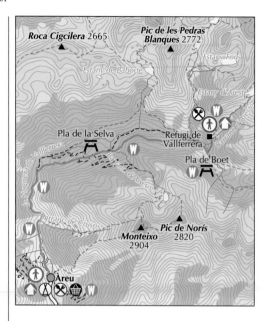

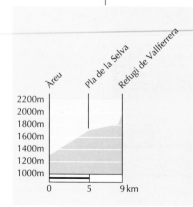

right of the meadow to reach a larger track. Turn left along this to reach the dirt road, at a signed junction. Turn right and immediately left. At the next meeting with the dirt road, turn left along it and then fork left at the **Pla de la Selva**, which has a picnic site (1hr 50min, 1695m). A sign here reminds you that you are only allowed to camp between 8pm and 8am.

A few minutes later fork right on a path which joins a track as it contours through the forest high above the river. Eventually (2hr 35min) fork right up a path and follow this to the large car park at La Molinassa (2hr 55min). Keep straight on at the top of the car park, shortcutting the last switchback on the track, then follow the track. Five minutes later there is

a left turn across a bridge (3hr, 1840m) signed to the Refugi
de Vallferrera.

The GR11 continues up the Vall Ferrera and doesn't
actually visit the refuge. If you don't need the refuge continue along the track and start Stage 30. Otherwise turn left
and follow the good path to the **Refugi de Vallferrera** (3hr
15min, 1920m, N42°37.500 E001°23.272).

Refugi de Vallferrera offers a full refuge service.
Open June to October.

Facilities on Stage 29
Refugi de Vallferrera: tel 973 624 378

STAGE 30
Refugi de Vallferrera to Refugi de Comapedrosa

Start	Refugi de Vallferrera
Distance	10km
Total Ascent	900m
Total Descent	500m
Difficulty	There is much boulderfield and some scree on this crossing of a high alpine pass. The route would be a serious undertaking in bad weather or early in the season when there will be a lot of snow. The ascent in snow would only be for properly equipped, experienced mountaineers. Start early in the morning so you cross the pass before any possible afternoon thunderstorms. Navigation will be difficult in poor visibility.
Time	5hr 5min
High Point	Portella de Baiau (2757m)

Today's scenic route is a demanding crossing of the Portella de Baiau from Spain
into Andorra. It would be possible to continue down to the ski resort of Arinsal
(see Stage 31) for full tourist facilities.

Pla de Baiau

The **Vall Ferrera**, like many valleys on the border between France and Spain, has seen a lot military action with border raids being a common occurrence in the past. In 1597 a French army of 2000 Lutherans crossed the Port de Boet and sacked the villages of Vall Ferrera, a massacre out of proportion to the normal raids. The Republican Pyrenees Battalion was based here during the Spanish Civil War and they prepared a route over the snow-covered Port de Boet to allow Republican soldiers and civilians to escape to France after defeat by the Fascist army of Franco.

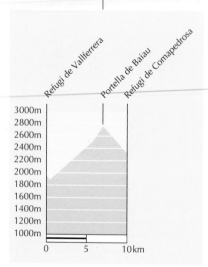

Return to the main track in the Vall Ferrera. The GR11 continues along the track to reach the **Pla de Boet** (10min, 1850m). Picnic site, water-point, camping and toilets, whose condition in 2013 suggested maintenance problems. There is good camping with water at regular intervals all the way to the Refugi de Baiau.

The GR11 stays on the track to the right of the Pla de Boet. The waymarking isn't very good ahead, but look out for cairns when waymarks are missing. Leave the track at a switchback, keeping straight on to arrive at the meadows of the Pla d'Arcalis (40min, 2000m). Stay right of the stream as you pass through a semi-wooded area of the meadow, heading roughly SE and gradually veering E, to reach a flat grassy area, **Pla de Baiau** (1hr 15min, 2130m). The path crosses the stream here and veers round the left-hand side of the rocky

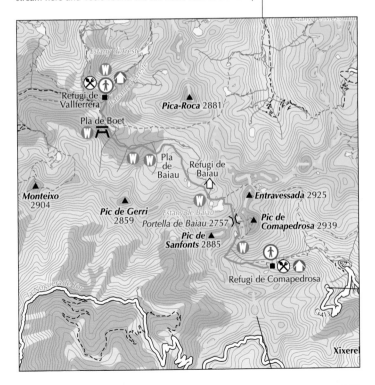

Refugi de Baiau

ridge ahead and climbs easily, veering SSE, up its grassy NE flank to reach the Estanys d'Escorbes (2hr 10min, 2360m). The path continues roughly SE to the Estany de Baiau (lower lake) from where you climb to the **Refugi de Baiau** (2hr 45min, 2517m, N42°35.851 E001°25.749) on the rocky knoll on your left. The well-maintained, purpose-built bothy of Refugi de Baiau has nine bunks.

From the hut go E down a gully and veer left across rock before you descend to the N end of **Estany de Baiau** (upper lake). Last campsites on the ascent. Head along the shore, cross a boulderfield, then follow the path which heads away from the lake. At the top of a grassy slope keep straight on across a little valley, veering to the right to follow a route through the boulderfields and scree. Relatively good paths are developing and the going is fairly easy until you get to the final steeper slopes, just below the col. Waymarking seems designed for those descending rather than climbing so if you look back you can often pick up the line better. Reach the **Portella de Baiau** (4hr 5min, 2757m, N42°35.558 E001°26.322) and enter Andorra. Remember that the camping laws are the same as in Spain. Fires are not permitted! ◄

It would be possible to climb Pic de Comapedrosa (2939m) from here, ascending the NW ridge and descending the obvious scree path on the W face.

Descend easily SSE, soon veering right past the two Estany Negre lakes. Cross the outlet of the lower lake and follow the path down the right-hand side of the valley into the Coma Pedrosa, a classic hanging valley. This valley provides the only good wild camping during the descent. You reach a path junction (4hr 55min) where you fork right to the **Refugi de Comapedrosa** on a shelf just above the valley floor (5hr 5min, 2260m, N42°34.631 E001°27.032). The left fork is the old route of the GR11, which you could follow if you don't want the refuge.

> Refugi de Comapedrosa is a modern manned refuge with full refuge facilities. It is open June to the end of September.

Facilities on Stage 30
Refugi de Comapedrosa: tel (00376) 327 995

STAGE 31
Refugi de Comapedrosa to Arans

Start	Refugi de Comapedrosa
Distance	9km
Total Ascent	500m
Total Descent	1400m
Difficulty	Easy
Time	3hr 50min
High Point	Refugi de Comapedrosa (2260m), Coll de les Cases (1958m)

An easy descent down to the ski resort Arinsal is followed by a steep crossing of the S ridge of Pic de Percanela at the Coll de les Cases. It would be possible to continue into Stage 32 and stay overnight at Ordino.

Turn left, downhill from the refuge, then right at a junction to regain the old route of the GR11. Continue down the right-hand side of the Riu de Pedrosa, eventually crossing it and the Riu d'Areny on bridges and soon reaching a track at the boundary of the National Park (55min).

Almost immediately fork right and follow the track down to the avalanche wall which crosses the valley. The track is forced right and becomes a tarmac road – follow this across the river. Turn left through the road tunnel under the avalanche wall to arrive at the top of **Arinsal** (1hr 15min). Fork left down the road, passing several water-points to the main facilities in the ski resort, which are about 1km down the road. Continue down the main street until a mini-roundabout just after the second supermarket where there is a road on the left signed 'El Mas de Ribafeta'. Follow the road as it switchbacks up the hill until, at the top, a footpath 'Cami del Coll de la Cases' goes off left at a bend (1hr 45min). Follow this good path steeply up to the **Coll de les Cases** (3hr, 1958m, N42°34561 E001°30.017). Good dry campsites. ◄

There is a waymarked path left from here to Pic de Percanela (2494m).

Arinsal is a ski resort which seems to stay fully open in the summer. There are numerous hotels, bars and restaurants to choose between, as well as two supermarkets and other shops. The speciality seems

Camping at Coll de les Cases

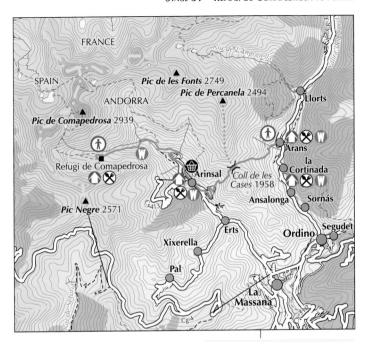

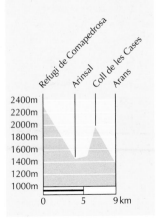

to be 'pubs' to cater for the large British and Irish population as well as the tourists. Esports St. Moritz stocks 'Coleman-style' camping gas.

Follow the well-marked path steeply downhill, ignoring a few sideturns. Cross a stream at the foot of the forest (3hr 35min) and climb a little, staying in the woods, before descending again and completing the descent on a track to reach a tarmac road. Turn right, switchbacking down, with waymarked shortcuts, to pass a water-point and reach the 'centre' of **Arans** on the main road (3hr 50min, 1360m, N42°34.928 E001°31.225).

Arans is a small hamlet with two hotels with bar-restaurants (Hotel Antic and Aparthotel Arans), but no shop.

Facilities on Stage 31
Hotel Antic: tel (00376) 850 988
Aparthotel Arans: tel (00376) 850 111 www.aparthotelarans.com

STAGE 32
Arans to Encamp

Start	Arans
Distance	12km
Total Ascent	1200m
Total Descent	1300m
Difficulty	Easy
Time	5hr 20min
High Point	Coll d'Ordino (1983m)

The route on Stage 31 from Arisal to Arans and its continuation on Stage 32 manage to find a quiet route avoiding the noise, congestion and supermarkets of the main towns of Andorra.

Cross the main road and go down the road opposite the Hotel Arans to cross the river. Then turn right along a track, signed to La Cortinada, which becomes a path before reaching a tarmac road. Cross the bridge here and turn left down the main road to reach **La Cortinada** (10min). If you want the centre of the hamlet keep on down the road.

La Cortinada is a hamlet with several hotels (including Hotel Sveara) and bar-restaurants, but no shop.

The GR11 goes left across a bridge. Water-point on the left. Continue along an old cobbled street before reaching the next bridge, where you could turn right to Hotel Sveara.

The GR11 takes the road left of the par 3 golf course. Water-point on the left. The road soon becomes a track, then a path. Fork left, signed to Les Planes de Sornas, and climb steeply with switchbacks until you reach a ridge (50min). There are dry camping possibilities here or ahead. Contour above some meadows with barns and keep straight on at a junction, following a sign to Ordino. In this section there are lots of side paths, but you follow the waymarked main path. Cross a stream (1hr) and start climbing again to cross a broad ridge (1hr 15min). From here you descend a little before climbing to and up another ridge (2hr). Then descend steeply to a track and turn right, signed to Ordino (2hr 10min). Descend switchbacks to a track junction at a stream

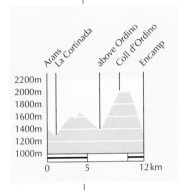

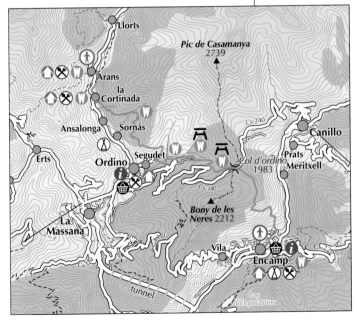

Font de le Navina

crossing. Turn right and 100m later turn left up a path signed to Coll d'Ordino (2hr 25min). Go straight on here if you need Ordino, about 10min away.

> Ordino is a tourist village with a tourist informa-
> tion office, lots of hotels, a small range of shops and
> campground.

Turn right at a junction (2hr 35min) then turn left along a track (2hr 45min) and almost immediately cross a stream and fork left up a path. This path soon crosses a track and climbs to reach a picnic area, with a water catchment res-ervoir which might pass as a rather chilly swimming pool (3hr 50min). Turn right down the track and then fork left up a smaller track which may have a chain across it. This track veers left before forking left and left again along a path which leads to a second picnic site at the Font de la Navina (3hr 40min). Water-point. Fork left up a path immediately above the picnic area and join a track which becomes a path to reach the road and car park at the **Coll d'Ordino** (4hr 5min, 1983m, N42°33.347 E001°34.265).

> **Bony de les Neres** (2212m) to the SW is an easy walk, but unfortunately the summit is dominated by a communications complex (30min up, 20min down). **Pic de Casamanya** (2739m) to the N is a much more worthwhile climb. There is a good path all the way to the summit (100min up, 55min down).

Cross the road and follow a grass path to an 'orientation table' and signpost. Follow signs, roughly SE, to Encamp les Bons. Take care, as there are other paths from the orientation table. Ignore a turn to Ríu d'Urina Racons as you cross grassland. Excellent dry campsites. Take care to follow the waymarks, as there are several other paths in the area. Once you are descending through the woods go left at a signed junction (4hr 35min) and then cross a small stream several times lower down the descent. Near the bottom you pass a ruined castle and the old chapel just above the town of **Encamp** (5hr 10min).

> **Torre de los Moros** (tower of the Moors) is the remains of a larger fort which would have dominated the area in medieval days. The Lombard Romanesque Church of Sant Romà de les Bons was consecrated in 1164.

Continue down to a tarmac road, Carrer de St Romà. Water-point. Follow this road as it switchbacks down to and across the Pont de les Bons. Veer right (WSW) down the Avingudo de Rouillac to reach a main road. Cross the main road and go down some steps, straight on to the left of the La Mosquera Bar-restaurant and down Carrer de la Girauda to arrive at the tourist information office (5hr 20min) with a supermarket opposite. There are more shops, hotels and bar-restaurants further down, as well as a campground.

> Encamp is a town with all facilities for tourists, including a campground. Tèchnic Esports, to the SE of the town, is a good outdoor store and stocks all types of camping gas. There is a bus link to Barcelona and Barcelona Airport. Camping Internacional has cabins and bar-restaurant.

Facilities on Stage 32
Hotel Sveara: tel (00376) 850 151
Ordino Tourist Office: tel (00376) 878 173 www.ordino.ad
Encamp Tourist Office: tel (00376) 731 000 www.encamp.ad
Camping Internacional: tel (00376) 831 609 www.campinginternacional.com

STAGE 33

Encamp to Refugio de l'Illa

Start	Encamp
Distance	15km
Total Ascent	1500m
Total Descent	300m
Difficulty	Easy
Time	5hr 25min
High Point	Coll Jovell (1779m), Refugio de l'Illa (2485m)

The 2-day crossing back into Catalonia is the final alpine section of the GR11. This stage ends at an unmanned refuge and is a problem for those who require manned accommodation. The next en-route accommodation is at the Refugi de Malniu at the end of Stage 34, after about 11 hours of walking. Those requiring accommodation should follow the alternative route (GR11-10) via Refugi Xalet Cap del Rec, as described in Stages 33A and 34A.

Go down the road to the left of the tourist office and fork left up Carrer de Sant Miquel. Turn right at the end of the road and fork left up Cami de l'Arena. Veer slightly right across a roundabout and down a track. Don't be surprised if future building changes the detail here. Turn left at a junction and climb to the new 'bypass' at a roundabout. Cross and climb steps, signed to Llac d'Engolasters, and follow an old path. Keep straight on at a junction by an electricity pylon and follow signs left at the next pylon (15min). Follow GR markings as you climb, ignoring a number of sideturns, until you pass a large building (50min). Immediately after this building there are dry campsites on a flat semi-wooded area on your right. Continue climbing to reach the E end of **Estany d'Engolasters** where there are two bar-restaurants (1hr 10min, 1616m, 42°31.334 E001°34.328).

Follow the track along the S shore of the reservoir, forking left up a tarmac road at the dam, and follow this road to the second switchback, where there is a car park and information office (1hr 30min). Head roughly SW past the information office along a track signed 'Camé del Matxos'.

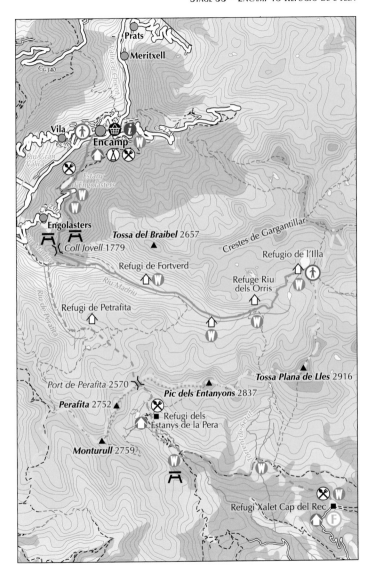

Vall de Riu Madriu

This track contours and soon passes the Font de les Ordigues. Water. Pass through a short tunnel, pass a viewpoint and reach the Font de les Mollere. Water. This track ends at a picnic site with an open shelter (1hr 45min). The water point here is likely to be dry. Continue along the 'tourist' path, ignoring a couple of side turns, as it climbs gently to **Coll Jovell** where there is a picnic table (2hr 5min, 1779m, N42°30.098 E001°33.827). Continue down a good path on the other side, signed 'Cami dels Matxos'. At the bottom pass a rough hut, which could serve as an emergency shelter, just before a signed junction (2hr 25min, 1638m, N42°29.871 E001°34.450).

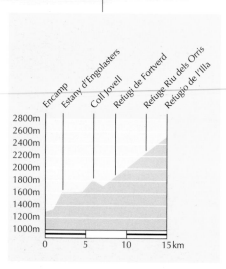

Turn sharp right if you are following the variation via Refugi Xalet Cap del Rec (Stages 33A and 34A). The GR11 goes straight on and climbs steadily, ignoring several side turns. Pass a house (2hr 45min) before arriving at the **Refugi de Fortverd** (3hr 5min). This is a modern well-maintained unmanned refuge with piped water outside. The old hut just below is also useable. This is where you will find the first good campsites in the valley. There are frequent excellent campsites throughout the remainder of the section.

Continue climbing past a small hut, suitable for emergency use only, and immediately afterwards fork left, staying left of the main stream (3hr 30min). Ignore a log bridge on the right (4hr 10min) which leads to a basic bothy across the stream on the right. Continue to the **Refuge Riu dels Orris** (4hr 30min, 2230m), a small bothy in good condition in 2013. Soon after this pass a farmer's hut, after which the path veers left away from the stream. You pass another small hut and a few ponds as the path winds between granite knolls. Cross a stream (5hr 15min) and eventually reach the **Refugio de l'Illa** (5hr 25min, 2485m, N42°29.618 E001°39.387). This unmanned refuge is very much a superior bothy with three large rooms. Piped water outside. ▶

See Stage 34 if you want to climb a peak from the refuge.

Shepherd's hut below Refugi de l'Illa

STAGE 33A
Encamp to Refugi Xalet Cap del Rec

Start	Encamp
Distance	25km
Total Ascent	1800m
Total Descent	1000m
Difficulty	Fairly easy mountain paths
Time	8hr 20min
High Point	Coll Jovell (1779m), Port de Perafita (2570m)

It would be possible to split this long day by staying at the Refugi dels Estanys de la Pera.

For route map see Stage 33.

◄ Follow the GR11 (Stage 33) as far as the junction 15min after Coll Jovell (2hr 25min). Turn sharp right down the GR7 and descend to a signed junction by farm buildings at Entremesaigües (2hr 40min). Turn left, signed 'Camí de Perafita', cross the bridge and veer left up the left bank of the **Riu de Perafita**. A good mountain path takes you up this rough, steep valley to reach a very basic bothy when the gradient eases at the top of the forest. Keep straight on and soon reach the **Refugi de Perafita** (4hr 40min, 2200m, N42°28.779 E001°34.702), a small, maintained unmanned refuge. Good campsites. There is water, but it might dry up in a long dry spell. Follow the GR11-10, signed to Port de Perafita. The path is extremely faint, but the waymarks are fairly good. You are heading roughly SE before veering right as you approach the ridge. The col isn't the obvious steep col ahead but the gentler **Port de Perafita** hidden away on the right (5hr 55min, 2570m, N42°27.912 E001°35.638). ◄

Pic dels Entanyons (2837m) to the E, and Perafita (2752m) and Monturull (2759m) to the SW are easy climbs.

The descent path is clear and takes you easily down to the manned **Refugi dels Estanys de la Pera** (6hr 20min, 2335m, N42°27.389 E001°35.939).

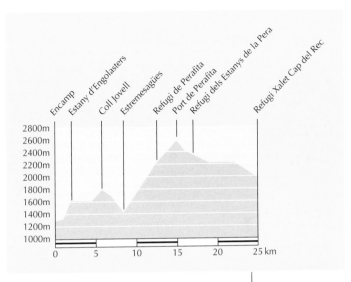

Looking down Val de Perafita

189

Refugi dels Estanys de la Pera, with full refuge facilities, is open from mid June to mid September and weekends at other times of year.

Head S from the refuge until you meet a dirt road, then take a series of shortcuts as the road switchbacks down to a junction (6hr 30min). Turn left. Right would take you to a large picnic area, water-point and shelter. The road now contours through pleasant forest to the (locked) Refugio del Pradell (7hr 40min). Veer right off the track to pick up a path entering the wood at the far left of the pasture. Follow the well-marked complex route to **Refugi Xalet Cap del Rec** (8hr 20min, 1987m, N42°25.868 E001°40.085).

Refugi Xalet Cap del Rec has full refuge facilities. It is open all year. As well as the refuge there is a water-point, separate bar-restaurant, large car park and cross-country ski school.

Facilities on Stage 33
Refugi dels Estanys de la Pera: tel 606 991 473 www.feec.cat
Refugi Xalet Cap del Rec: tel 973 293 050

STAGE 34

Refugio de l'Illa to Refugio de Malniu

Start	Refugio de l'Illa
Distance	14km
Total Ascent	1000m
Total Descent	1300m
Difficulty	There is some rough going. Although the route is well waymarked, care would be needed with navigation in poor visibility. The descent from Portella d'Engorgs could be dangerous in snow.
Time	5hr 15min
High Point	Coll de Vall Civera (2550m), Portella d'Engorgs (2680m)

Although the valleys still have an alpine feel, the ridges have more of a Scottish Highland feel to them. There are camping opportunities and water throughout this section.

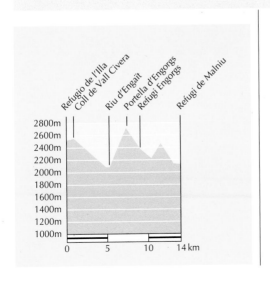

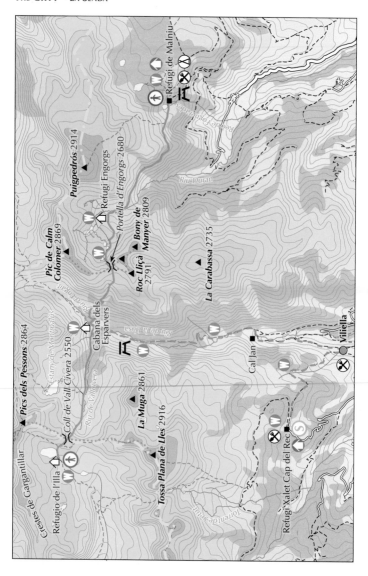

Follow the path to the right end of the dam just above the refuge and continue on the same line to a signpost above the reservoir.

> **Pic dels Pessons** (2864m) to the N is an easy peak from here. Follow the GR7 until it contours left of the summit then just head up the ridge to the summit (55min up, 35min down). Tossa Plana de Lles (2916m), to the S, also looks straightforward.

The GR7 forks left and the GR11 right, to reach the grassy **Coll de Vall Civera** (15min, 2550m, N42°29.618 E001°39.738). This is where we leave Andorra and re-enter Catalonia. Follow the well-marked path steeply down the other side to the valley floor and then down the left-hand bank of the **Riu de Vallcivera**, to reach the **Cabana dels Esparvers** in a large meadow as you approach the bottom of the valley. The original 'cabana', on the right of the path, looks like an ancient burial mound and you wouldn't want to use it. The newer 'cabana' still looks very old, but is a sounder structure and could be used for 2–3 people

Camp on descent from Coll de Vall Civera

overnight. However, it is rather rough and many walkers would only consider it for emergencies (1hr 25min, 2068m, N42°29.123 E001°42.190).

Ascend a small rise E, then descend slightly left to a signpost and turn right (E) across the **Riu d'Engaït**. Follow the well-waymarked route up lightly wooded pasture. Cross a small stream (1hr 55min) which was running in late July 2012. Good camping and water. Continue climbing to reach the floor of a small corrie (2hr 40min), climb steeply out of it and then veer left up a grassy hillside to the broad **Portella d'Engorgs** (3hr 15min, 2680m, N42°28.859 E001°43.591).

You could climb **Pic de Calm Colomer** (2869m) to the N from here. Easy scrambling is required on the shattered rocky ridge, but all the difficulties can be avoided by staying below the ridge on the SE face (45min up, 30min down). If you want easier summits you could climb Roc Lliçà (2791m) to the SSW of the col and then traverse Bony de Manyer Nord (2806m) en route for Bony de Manyer (2809m). The round trip is about 1hr. There is a curious 'border' stone on the summit of Bony de Manyer inscribed with the Roman XV.

West top, Bony de Manyer

You should stick to the well-marked path down a short steep descent to reach a shallow lake then veer right over boulderfield to further lakes, the Estany dels Aparellats. You need to keep a close eye on the cairns and waymarks in mist as the path is very indistinct. Continue roughly E to the **Refugi Engorgs**, a small unmanned bothy which was in good condition in 2013 (3hr 40min, 2380m, N42°28.875 E001°44.734).

Head SSE from the refuge, cross the stream and head up a slight rise the other side. The path is unclear; it doesn't head up the ridge, but follows a line above the stream. There will probably be several streams running in the next section. The path now becomes well defined, but rather rough, and you follow it as it traverses the steep S slopes of Puigpedrós (2914m) and climbs steadily to reach a grassy ridge (4hr 50min, 2320m, N42°27.838 E001°46.217). Follow the path to the **Refugi de Malniu** (5hr 15min, 2138m, N42°27.854 E001°47.162) which you can see beside a small lake ESE from here.

> Refugi de Malniu provides a full refuge service. There is also a car park, toilet block, picnic area, water-point, basic campground (for which there is a small fee) and permanent orienteering course. Open mid-June to mid-September and some weekends outside this period.

Facilities on Stage 34
Refugi de Malniu: tel 616 855 535 www.refugimalniu.com

STAGE 34A

Refugi Xalet Cap del Rec to Refugio de Malniu (GR11-10)

Start	Refugi Xalet Cap del Rec
Distance	21km
Total Ascent	1500m
Total Descent	1300m
Difficulty	Easy until after the GR11 (Stage 34) has been rejoined.
Time	7hr 35min
High Point	Portella d'Engorgs (2680m)

This is a continuation of Stage 33A and you are following the GR11-10 until you rejoin the GR11 at the Cabana dels Esparvers.

For route map
see Stage 34.

◄ Follow the track roughly ESE from the refuge. Take care at the first junction, as a twisted signpost could be confusing.

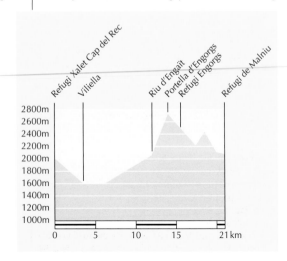

Follow the well-marked, complex route all the way to **Viliella** (1hr 5min, 1600m, N42°24.928 E001°41.774), a small hamlet with a bar-restaurant but no other facilities for hikers. Turn sharp left below the church and follow a good track to **Cal Jan de la Llosa** (1hr 45min). Veer right in front of the farm buildings, cross the river and turn left up an old walled lane. You soon turn left up a good track. Fork right (2hr 45min) before reaching a bridge over the **Riu de la Llosa** (3hr 15min). Excellent campsites here and further upstream. Pass a picnic table by a small shrine, soon after which the track gives way to a clear path which is followed to a bridge over the Riu de Vallcivera (3hr 45min, 2062m, N42°29.084 E001°42.149) just below the **Cabana dels Esparvers**. Cross the stream and veer right to follow the GR11 to the **Refugio de Malniu**, as described in Stage 34 (7hr 35min).

STAGE 35
Refugi de Malniu to Puigcerdà

Start	Refugi de Malniu
Distance	14km
Total Ascent	100m
Total Descent	1100m
Difficulty	Easy
Time	3hr 10min
High Point	E top, Roc Roig (2170m)

This is an easy downhill section to reach the high plateau around Puigcerdà.

Cross the bridge on the track immediately below the refuge and then turn left along a path. Follow the GR11 waymarks carefully, as there are more prominent local paths. The GR11 joins local path 120 and veers right, gradually climbing the gentle ridge to reach a large grassy area (30min) with a dirt road visible ahead. Veer left along the edge of the grassy area, now local path 139, turning left along the dirt road to reach a signpost at the beginning of another large grassy area, the

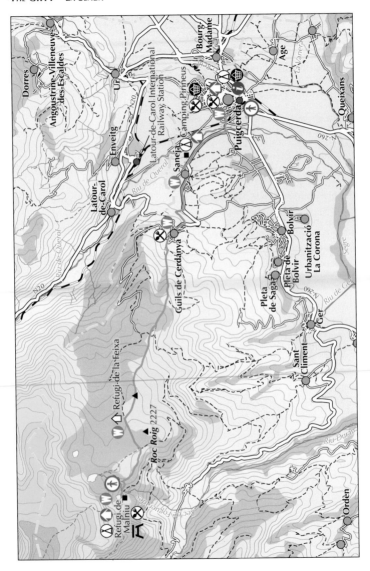

Descent from Refugi de la Feixa

Pla de la Feixa (40min). The bothy **Refugi de la Feixa** is just ahead on your left with a water-point 100m beyond it. This bothy was in excellent condition in 2013.

Turn diagonally right across the short grass, veering slightly right (SE), then left (E) to pick up a faint grassy track which takes you to the E top of **Roc Roig** (50min, 2170m, N42°27.600 E001°49.271). It is now downhill all the way to Puigcerdà. Descend easily on pasture through woodland to a dirt road. Keep straight on across this road, now local path 200, and follow a track through the woods to an area clear-felled after being destroyed by fire in 2012. Waymarks were still missing in 2013. Keep going down the

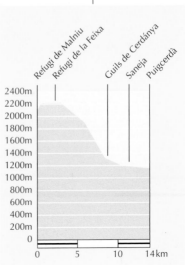

ridge to leave the fire-damaged area and reach a signpost in a grassy area (1hr 35min). The last camping opportunity on the descent.

Continue down the now stonier ridge to reach a track just above **Guils de Cerdánya**. Follow the track which soon becomes a tarmac road. Veer left down to a junction and turn right. The Font de la Canal is on your left. Fork left, passing another water-point, and descend to a junction where a road with a GR waymark goes left across a bridge. ◀ The GR11 continues down, by-passing the bar-restaurant! At the bottom of the hamlet veer left across the stream and reach the 'main' road (GIV-4035) (2hr 5min). Follow this road, then turn left up a track by a 5km sign, and turn right at a junction to return to the main road. Turn left and then left into **Saneja**. Water-point on the left. Keep straight on to reach the church (2hr 40min, 1220m), then veer right back to the main road and turn left.

> The left turn leads, by a complex route, down to Latour-de-Carol in France.

Camping Pirineus has cabins, bar-restaurant and a shop which stocks 'original' and 'Coleman-style' camping gas.

Pass **Camping Pirineus** and continue to St. Martí d'Aravó (3hr), then turn left to cross the bridge and enter **Puigcerdà**. Follow the road right to a roundabout. Water-point on the left. Turn left across the railway to a Fiat garage and turn right down this commercial road to reach the railway station (3hr 10min, 1204m, N42°25.774 E001°55.493).

Puigcerdà is a town with all facilities, most of which are at the top of the hill. Butano Cerdánya, in Carrer Font d'en Lleres, stocks all types of camping gas. There are many hotels and hostals – the three closest to the station are listed. There are rail links to Barcelona, Toulouse and Perpignan from Puigcerdà.

Facilities on Stage 35
Camping Pirineus: tel 972 881 062 www.stel.es
Hostal Estació: tel 972 880 350
Hotel Tèrminus: tel 972 880 212 www.hotelterminus.net
Hotel Puigcerdà: tel 972 882 181 www.hotelpuigcerda.cat
Puigcerdà Tourist Office: tel 972 880 542 www.puigcerda.cat

STAGE 36

Puigcerdà to Camping Can Fosses, Planoles

Start	Puigcerdà
Distance	25km
Total Ascent	1200m
Total Descent	1100m
Difficulty	Easy walking, but care is needed with navigation as some of the waymarking is only just adequate.
Time	6hr 25min
High Point	Coll de Marcer (1980m), Coll de la Creu de Meians (2000m)

The 'alpine' mountains are now behind us and next three days are through the high but gentler mountains which form the border between Spain and France. Don't be lulled into complacency, these mountains seem to attract more than their fair share of terrific thunderstorms.

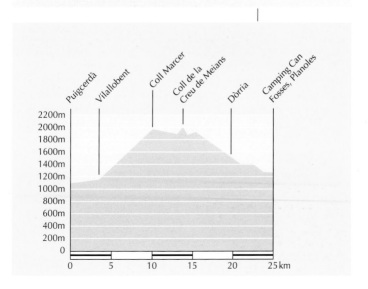

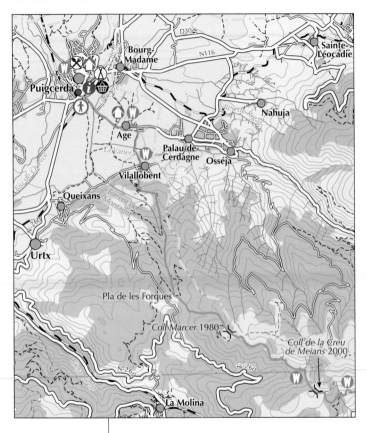

map continues
on page 205

From the station, keep straight on (SE) past a petrol station to a large roundabout. Cross and turn left, then first right down Camí d'Age and then veer left down the road signed to Age and Vilallobent. Don't get confused by GR4 waymarks. The GR11 goes through **Age** (25min), but it is possible to use the bypass to the S of the hamlet. Water-point left from the main square, Placa Major.

Age has a 'Turisme Rural' called Cal Marrufès.

202

Veer right as you leave the hamlet and keep straight on (S) to **Vilallobent** (45min, 1170m). Water-point in the park on the right. The GR11 continues S up a concrete track which soon turns to gravel. As this veers right, the GR11 forks left up a rough track. This shortcut eventually returns to the better track (1hr). Turn left, then fork right up another shortcut, turning right on returning to the main track. Fork right, then left up the main track (1hr 20min) and eventually fork right up a path (1hr 55min) to cross the Torrent de Montagut, which may be dry and, if running, would need treating before drinking. There are good dry campsites as you follow the 'stream' up, and plenty of campsites all the way to the Torrent del Pla de les Salines. You reach some tracks on the ridge at the **Pla de les Forques** (2hr 10min, 1719m, N42°22.370 E001°57.750). Turn left (SE) along the second of these tracks and continue up to a sharp right-hand bend (2hr 40min). Turn left up a probably dried up stream to a signpost on the ridge (2hr 50min) just below Border Stone 500 (N42°21.718 E001°59.184) at the **Coll Marcer**.

Contour into a wood where a recently 'improved' track should be obvious and follow this track past a succession of

Coll Marcer

border stones, starting with Stone 501, to a stream by Border Stone 501-VI (3hr 30min). Ignore the track dropping down to the right and climb gently to Border Stone 502 on a grassy ridge at **Coll de la Creu de Meians** (3hr 40min, 2000m, N42°20.826 E002°00.968).

The signs and waymarking here are confusing.

◄ Head ESE then veer SSE down a boggy gully to reach a track (3hr 50min). The GR11 is waymarked but if you lose the route just head down, roughly SE, to the track below. Turn left along the track to reach a junction. Turn left and then immediately right along a path, crossing a small stream which will probably be running. The path contours below the main track which it approaches at Torrent Llarg (4hr 10min), but it continues below the track to join it further along (4hr 20min). Turn right along the track and descend. There are two shortcuts on the left as the track starts switchbacking down to the Torrent del Pla de Les Salines (4hr 55min). This steam looks as if it will flow through the summer. Camping is possible.

Fork right and reach **Dòrria** (5hr 10min). There is a water-point and seating area beside the church. The GR11 does not enter Dòrria but continues along a concrete track

Church at Dòrria

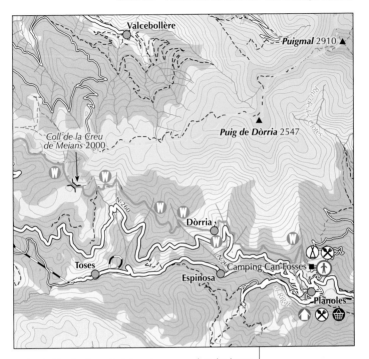

and switchbacks down to join a tarmac road at the lower
end of Dòrria. Almost immediately turn sharp left (N) down
a track and then turn right down a path immediately before
a stream. There are lots of terraced fields with numerous
side paths, but keep to the 'main' path which just about has
enough waymarks. The path stays roughly level as it traverses
above the road to reach an open ridge (5hr 40min). The path
has become a track by the time you reach a signpost at Serrat
de Mestre (6hr 5min, 1272m, N42°19.446 E002°05.866). If
you want Planoles turn right down the concrete track.

> Planoles has a variety of accommodation, several
> small shops and bar-restaurants. Hotel Rural Can
> Cruells is on the N-152 just E of Planoles.

The GR11 goes left on a track, crossing a stream, turning right and then forking left (6hr 20min) to reach a signpost immediately after some big water-tanks (6hr 25min, 1300m, N42°19.433 E002°06.213). If you don't want **Camping Can Fosses** you can turn left here and start Stage 37. Otherwise keep straight on along a path which drops down to the campground in a couple of minutes (1270m).

Camping Can Fosses also has cabins and bar-restaurant.

Facilities on Stage 36
Cal Marrufès: tel 972 141 174 www.calmarrufes.com
Hotel Rural Can Cruells: tel 972 736 399 http://cruells.cat/en
Cal Gasparó: tel 972 736 192 www.gasparo.cat
Hostal Cal Daldó: tel 972 736 133
Hostel Planoles – 'Pere Figuera': tel 972 736177
Camping Can Fosses: tel 972 736 065 www.canfosses.com

STAGE 37
Camping Can Fosses, Planoles to Núria

Start	Camping Can Fosses
Distance	18km
Total Ascent	1600m
Total Descent	900m
Difficulty	Easy. Adequate waymarking to Queralbs, after which Núria is well signed.
Time	5hr 55min
High Point	Collet de les Barraques (1890m), Creu d'en Riba (1983m)

This stage takes you up the spectacular Gorges de Núria, accompanied by hundreds of tourists. You could break the section as there is accommodation at Refugi Corral Blanc and Queralbs en route.

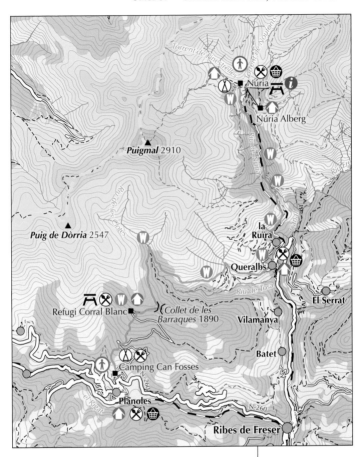

From Camping Can Fosses, return to the path junction by the water-tanks. The GR11 goes steeply uphill along a path, crosses a track and then a tarmac road. Next time you meet the road, turn right along it and then turn left on a bend. This steep path climbs easily through pleasant woodland. Fork left to reach a track, cross it and then the road to reach a large picnic site (1hr 10min). The lower water-point may be dry,

207

Gorges de Núria

but the higher one should be flowing. The manned **Refugi Corral Blanc** is just to the left of the picnic site.

> Refugi Corral Blanc has full refuge facilities and is open mid-June to mid-September and at weekends outside this period.

Continue up through the picnic area to the road and turn right along it to the car park at the roadhead at **Collet de les Barraques** (1hr 25min, 1890m, N42°20.309 E002°07.295). Turn left (NW) along a track and follow it until you reach a grassy area. This has the best dry campsites in this section. Fork right along a very faint waymarked path which becomes better defined as it gradually descends through the forest to the Torrent de l'Estremera (1hr 50min, 1800m). Cross the stream. Font de l'Home Mort is 100m upstream. You will find some small streams and possible campsites between Torrent de l'Estremera and Queralbs, but the quality of both may depend on the latest cow activity.

The GR11-8 goes left here while the GR11 goes right, soon forking right. Again there are too many side paths to describe, but follow the 'main' path and keep a close eye on the waymarks. The path becomes a bit vague across a grassy area, after which you pass a tiny hut, just about big

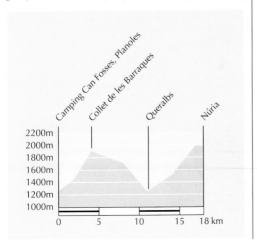

209

enough for two people to shelter in a storm. After the hut you descend below big cliffs and pass Font dels Plaus (2hr 30min) just before a farm building. Water. Reach a track and turn left (2hr 40min) and, soon after a switchback, take a shortcut left which regains the track just before a stream (2hr 45min). Turn left and continue along the track, forking right and then right again, ignoring a signpost suggesting you go left. Immediately after a switchback, turn sharp left down an old path to a concrete track (3hr). Turn left along a path which soon joins the concrete track. After the bell tower, turn sharp right to the church. Water-point. Turn sharp left and continue down through the centre of village of **Queralbs** and on to the main car park (3hr 10min, 1196m, N42°20.994 E002°09.804). Water-point.

Queralbs is a small village with a small shop and two Hostal bar-restaurants (Hostal L'Avet ca la Mari and Hostal Les Roquetes).

There are not very many GR waymarks in the next section but the route to Núria is very popular with tourists and

Catalan ass at Núria

is well signed. Imagination will be needed to find anywhere to camp before Núria. Follow a path steeply uphill, signed 'Cami de Núria', turning right and left onto a concrete road. After a few switchbacks, fork left up a concrete track which soon becomes a path. Turn right at a road, then fork left up a concrete track, forking left up a path just before a gate. Pass a water-point (3hr 30min). Follow signs to Pont de Cremel at a couple of junctions. You pass the 'Refugi St. Pau', a rock overhang under which you could shelter, before reaching the Pont de Cremel (4hr 10min). Cross the bridge and continue climbing the right-hand side of the gorge, passing the 'Refugi St. Rafael' (4hr 20min) and 'Refugi St. Pere' (5hr), two more rock overhangs. Cross a stream under a railway bridge (5hr 5min) and continue up the left-hand side of the valley. Eventually cross a ridge, Creu d'en Riba (5hr 45min, 1983m). ▶ Continue to **Núria** (5hr 55min, 1967m).

This is where you get your first view of Núria, which looks like a country house that has been transplanted into the mountains.

The Sanctuari de Núria is a holiday complex with hotel, youth hostel and basic campground. The shop has minimal food supplies. It is a ski resort in winter and a major tourist attraction in summer. Other attractions include pony trekking, a boating lake, picnic areas, play areas, an excellent interpretive centre, a cafeteria and a selection of bar-restaurants. Access is on foot or by the rack railway from Ribes de Freser or Queralbs.Hostel Núria (Alberg Pic de l'Àliga) is a short walk or cable car journey above Núria.

According to tradition, **Sant Gil** was a Greek who arrived in the valley in approximately 700AD and lived there for four years. He crafted an image of the Virgin Mary and later hid it in a cave when forced to flee from the Arians, a Christian sect. Legend has it that a pilgrim named Amadéu began searching for the image in 1072, after having a prophetic dream. He built a small chapel for pilgrims, and found the carving seven years later, and the place became known as the Sanctuary of the Virgin of Núria. The wooden Romanesque carving, which is still venerated today, has in fact been dated to about 1200.

It was in Núria that the first Catalan Statute of Autonomy was drafted in 1931, and Núria and the surrounding mountains are a popular destination for Catalans on their National Day, 11 September. This date commemorates the fall of Barcelona to the Bourbon king in 1714, which resulted in the incorporation of Catalonia into Castile in 1716, giving Spain a united administration.

Facilities on Stage 37
Refugi Corral Blanc: tel 626 274 395 www.corralblanc.com
Hostal L'Avet ca la Mari: tel 972 727 377
Hostal Les Roquetes: tel 972 727 369
Hotel Vall de Núria: tel 972 732 030 www.valldenuria.com
Hostel Núria (Alberg Pic de l'Àliga): tel 972 732 048
Núria Tourist Office: tel 972 732 020

STAGE 38
Núria to Setcases

Start	Núria
Distance	19km
Total Ascent	1100m
Total Descent	1800m
Difficulty	The walking is easy, but this is not a ridge for the inexperienced in bad weather. The ridge seems to attract afternoon thunder storms so it would be sensible to make an early morning start. Snow will be a problem early in the summer. Waymarking is good as far as the Refugi d'Ulldeter, after which it is sporadic.
Time	5hr 50min
High Points	Coll de Tirapits (2780m), Coll de la Marrana (2520m)

Surprisingly, well to the E of the high mountains, the GR11 attains its greatest height as it passes along the border ridge.

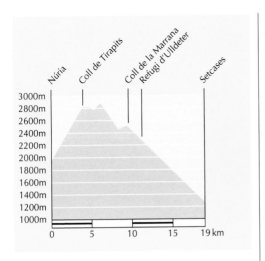

From the railway station at the NE corner of the Núria complex, head up the stream then turn right across an old bridge, signed 'GR11 Noucreus'. Climb diagonally up a bank and follow a path into the woods above the stream. This path soon climbs up to a track which you follow left, ignoring a right turn to 'Alberg' (the hostel) (20min). The track becomes a path by the time you pass the junction of the **Torrent de Noufonts** and Torrent de Noucreus. Cross the Torrent de Noucreus on a bridge. This may be your last water on the ascent. Head N to the right of the Torrent de Noufonts to reach a signpost.

Alternative route

The left turn, signed to Noufonts is the old route of the GR11 and it is suggested that you follow it in good weather. Follow the path up to the **Col de Noufonts** and turn right along the ridge to rejoin the GR11 at the **Coll de Noucreus**. This will add about 30min to the route. There is the added option of climbing the Pic de Noufonts (2861m) to the W of the Coll de Noufonts and the Pic de la Fossa between the two cols.

The GR11 goes right and follows the path above the left-hand bank of the Torrent de Noucreus. Eventually the path

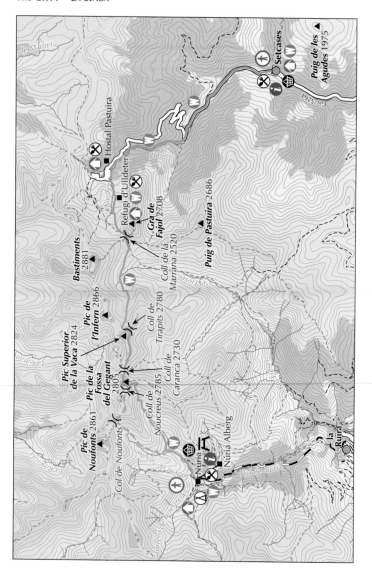

Puigmal from below Coll de Noucreus

crosses the 'torrent', by which time it may be dry, and then switchbacks up to the **Coll de Noucreus** (2hr 5min, 2785m, N42°25.047 E002°11.383) where nine small crosses are embedded in the rock.

> It is said that the **nine crosses** commemorate nine monks who died here when caught in a storm, but the evidence for this is rather sparse.

The GR11 goes slightly left of the easily climbed Pic de la Fossa del Gegant (2805m) with two more crosses. Descend E to **Coll de Caranca** (2730m) and climb to pass S of the summit of Pic Superior de la Vaca (2824m) to reach the **Coll de Tirapits** on its SE ridge (2hr 40min, 2780m, N42°24.934 E002°12.549).

The GR11 swings left (N) from here, forking right below an emergency shelter and then heading down to the left of the probably dry Torrent de les Barranques. Cross a stream (3hr 5min). The first water since the Torrent de Noucreus. There is plenty of camping between here and the Refugi de Ulldeter. Veer left down to a bigger stream where a variation,

215

Coll de Tirapits

Well-trod paths climb Gra de Fajol (2708m) to the SE and Bastiments (2881m) to the NW.

the GR11-7, joins from the right. The GR11 now makes a rising traverse to the **Coll de la Marrana** (3hr 35in, 2520m, N42°25.032 E002°14.531). ◄

Descend easily down a switchbacking path, then a well-waymarked broad path, ignoring a left fork, to reach a wide ski piste. Cross this and descend left of it down the ridge to the manned **Refugi d'Ulldeter** (4hr, 2220m, N42°25.179 E002°15.462). Water-point outside.

> Refugi d'Ulldeter, with full refuge facilities, is open from June to mid-September and weekends throughout the year.

A well-marked path goes left from the refuge before descending, crossing the stream and down a path, with many strands, to car parking on a switchback on the ski road (4hr 15min). The GR11 shortcuts the switchbacks on the road as you descend to the left of the stream and then follow the road until just below the bottom car park, then turn sharp right down a footpath signed 'GR11 Setcases' (4hr 30min). **Hostal Pastuira** is just down the road on the left.

Hostal Pastuira has alberg-style accommodation and a bar-restaurant.

The path veers left and joins a rough track which goes down the left-hand side of the **el Ter** stream. Pass the Font del Sauc, a small spring feeding a pipe on your right. Water. Good camping is in short supply in this rocky cow country, but you should be able to find somewhere to put a tent. Continue down the track until you reach the road at a switchback (5hr 5min). Follow this road down for 4km, passing a water-point on the left (5hr 20min). Continue to the Font del Pont Nou in a seating area immediately after the road crosses the el Ter (5hr 45min). Water. Ignore the right fork signed to Setcases and continue down the 'main' road to a parking area in **Setcases** (5hr 50min, 1265m, N42°22.543 E002°18.164). Most of the facilities in the village are on this road.

Setcases has two small food shops, lots of bar-restaurants and five hostal bar-restaurants offering accommodation (listed below).

Facilities on Stage 38
Refugi d'Ulldeter: tel 972 192 004 or 619 514 159 www.ulldeter.net
Hostal Pastuira: tel 972 136 043 www.pastuira.com
Setcases Tourist Information: tel 972 136 089
Hostal Restaurant Can Tiranda: tel 972 136 052 www.cantiranda.com
Hostal Restaurant la Cabanga: tel 972 136 065 www.lacabanya.es
Hostal Bar Restaurant El Moli: tel 972 136 049 www.elmoli.net
Hostal Restaurant Can Falera: tel 972 136 093
Hostal Restaurant Ter: tel 972 136 096 www.hostalter.com

STAGE 39
Setcases to Beget

Start	Setcases
Distance	21km
Total Ascent	1100m
Total Descent	1800m
Difficulty	Easy. Waymarking is generally good. The riverside path into Beget can be very slippery when wet.
Time	6hr 20min
High Point	Summit above Coll de Lliens (1904m)

The GR11 now leaves the high mountains and enters a region of steep wooded hills. As you are approaching the Mediterranean Sea you can expect hot dry conditions and you should be particularly careful not to start a wild-fire, as the woods are likely to be tinder-dry.

Looking back towards Núria from above Setcases

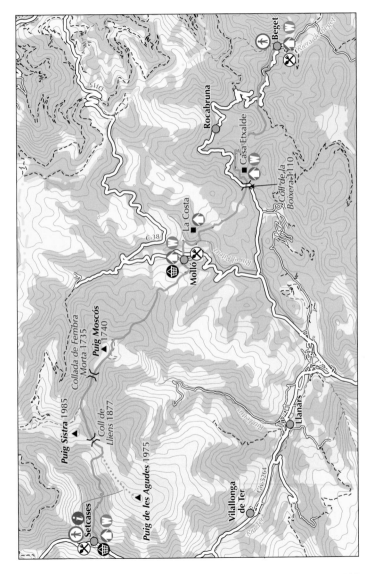

The GR11 crosses the Pont d'en Jepet, the bridge on the left, as you reach the village centre. Turn right past a water-point. Veer left on a concrete track which soon turns right over a bridge across the Torrent de Vall-Llobre. Follow a steep track which switchbacks up the hill. Ignore a path off on the right and a track which goes straight on at a switch-back. Continue climbing until a path goes off left (25min). Turn left along this path and after about 45min you pass through grassy areas. This is the first feasible dry camping on the ascent. You cross several small streams, but in this cow country the quality of the water could be a problem. Turn left (1hr 10min) and cross a large grassy area before joining a grassy track (1hr 20min). When you reach a large grassy area (1hr 25min) turn right straight up the hillside to reach a path (1hr 35min). Turn left and immediately right at the switchback of a grassy track and continue climbing. When you reach a grassy area just below the ridge, veer left along a line of poles. Excellent dry campsites. ◀

Puig de les Agudes (1975m) to the SW looks like an easy walk from here.

When you reach the fence, follow it left over a grassy top (1hr 50min, 1904m, N42°22.411 E002°20.271) and down to the **Coll de Lliens** (1877m) with a signpost. Cross the fence and go diagonally right along a path which contours the S face of Puig Sistra (1985m). Fork right (2hr 5min)

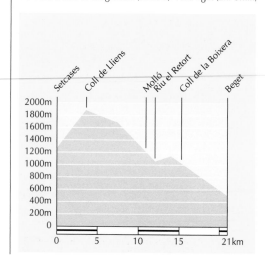

and ignore a path leading to the GR10 in France. On returning to the fence on the ridge, follow it down to the **Collada de Fembra Morta** (2hr 25min, 1735m) from where the path contours the S slopes of Puig Moscós. ▶

When you next meet the fence (2hr 30min), cross it and keep straight on to reach a fence on the next ridge (2hr 35min). Cross the fence and turn right along it, soon veering left down a track. This is the last of the good dry campsites. Fork right, then turn right after crossing another fence and continue roughly S down the ridge. Fork left to arrive at a junction just before a house (3hr 5min). Turn right along a track which soon becomes a concrete track. Turn left at a concrete road and sharp left down a tarmac road, and follow this down to the Font Vella at the NW end of **Molló** (3hr 25min, 1184m, N42°20.885 E002°24.230). Water-point.

> Molló has two small food shops, several bar-restaurants and an hotel (Hotel Can Calitxó).

Waymarking to Beget is sufficient to give you confidence you are on the right route, but not good enough to avoid possible problems at junctions. Follow the road up to Plaça Major and veer left down Carrer de Esglesia. At the bottom, cross the road and go down steps to the 'main' road, **C-38**. Cross and go diagonally left down a track, soon turning right down an old path, passing between two houses and continuing downhill to an old bridge across the **El Ritort** (3hr 40min, 1050m) with a swimming hole. Don't cross the bridge, but turn right and follow a concrete track downstream, past another bridge, through a farm and down to another bridge (3hr 45min) with bigger swimming holes. Continue on the track across the bridge and climb, ignoring sideturns.

Pass **La Costa**, which has accommodation. Keep straight on at the top of the hill and follow the track, which is grassy in places, to a track junction (4hr 20min) at the top of another hill. Follow the signpost, straight on, through the gate and across a field to another gate. Veer slightly left to cross a (dry) streambed, then E across the next field to pick up a path which reaches a track at a switchback. Fork right to the **Coll de la Boixera** (4hr 30min, 1110m, N42°19.817 E002°25.850).

Cross the road and take the path E into the woods descending to Can Serra. Water-point. You quickly reach

You could follow the fence over the summit of Puig Moscós (1740m) and regain the GR11 by its SE ridge.

Casa Etxalde with accommodation (4hr 45min). Follow the dirt road until a switchback when the GR11 goes straight on down a grass track (4hr 55min). If you lose the path you can pick up the track at the bottom right-hand corner of the field. Follow the track as it veers left before turning right along a major track which switchbacks down past Can Planas (5hr 10min, 830m). A couple of minutes later, when the dirt road goes sharp left, turn right down a path and veer left to farm buildings.

Continue down between the buildings and descend to cross a stream. Follow the path on the other side to a road (5hr 40min). Turn left and after 100m turn right down a path. This takes you down to the **Riera de Beget**, which you cross on an ancient bridge over a gorge. Follow the path downstream above the gorge, cross another ancient bridge and return to the road (6hr). Turn left down the road (GIV-5223). Take a path on the left at a right-hand bend and, ignoring any paths down to the river, follow the path to **Beget**. Follow the lower road to the village centre (6hr 20min). Two water-points.

Beget is a hamlet with one hostal and a bar-restaurant. Hostal el Forn is a bar-restaurant which offers accommodation in rooms at the hostal or apartments at Can Feliça.

GR11 hikers at Beget

Facilities on Stage 39
Hotel Can Calitxó: tel 972 740 386 www.hotelcalitxo.com
La Costa: tel 972 130 377 www.lacostademollo.com
Casa Etxalde: tel 972 130317 www.etxalde.net
Hostal el Forn: tel 972 741 230 www.elforndebeget.com

STAGE 40
Beget to Albanyà (via Sant Aniol d'Aguja)

Start	Beget
Distance	31km
Total Ascent	2200m
Total Descent	2500m
Difficulty	Easy walking, but limestone paths could be slippery when wet. Waymarking after Coll Roig is only just adequate.
Time	9hr 20min
High Point	Coll dels Muls (700m), Talaixà (760m), Coll Roig (840m), Coll de Principi (1126m).

The next section is a serious problem for those requiring accommodation. Earlier guides have split this section into two days, but the first day ended at Sant Aniol d'Aguja where there is no accommodation. There is the unmanned Refugi de Bassegoda en route. Those who are camping or bivouacking will almost certainly split this section into two days.

Follow the signs for GR11, veering right from the church and down a dirt road. Turn left when you reach the 'main' road and follow it across a bridge. Continue along the road to the next bridge (20min) and turn left up a concrete farm track, soon forking right and following the 'main' track, ignoring sideturns. Good dry campsites 30min from Beget. Fork right at a signed junction (40min), cross the river and bear left. When the track veers left, at La Farga, go straight on along a

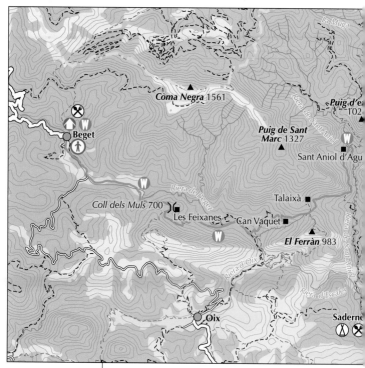

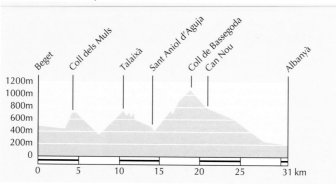

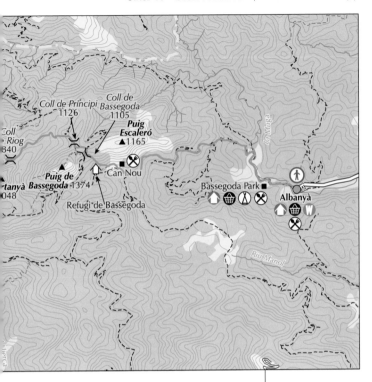

small path, cross a (dry) streambed and start climbing. Cross the **Coll dels Muls** (700m) and pass through **Les Feixanes**, a ruined farm (1hr 20min, 680m). Fork left and follow the main track, ignoring sideturns. Start switchbacking down to reach a large open area (1hr 40min). Good dry camping. Fork right at the bottom of the open area and continue descending, ignoring several tracks off to the left, to reach the **Riera de Beget** at some gates (1hr 55min). Follow the track to the right of the river. Pass through a grassy area with a (private) covered picnic area to the right. Pass a little spring on your right which, if running, will provide better quality water than that in the river. Water. Continue to a signpost by another grassy area, the **Pla de la Plantada** (2hr 5min, 370m), just before some gates. Camping is possible at either grassy area.

Sant Martí de Talaixà

Turn left, cross a bridge over the stream and follow the path which climbs to a track. Turn right and after a couple of minutes turn right up a path which looks more like a gully. Turn right at a track (2hr 40min) and follow switchbacks uphill to a ruined farmhouse, **Can Vaquet** (2hr 55min). Turn left up a path immediately before the farmhouse. Ignore lots of sideturns off this well-marked path and cross a track and climb to the pass at **Talaixà** (3hr 20min, 760m, N42°17.972 E002°34.353). There is a house, restored church, Sant Martí de Talaixà, and ruined village to the left of the trail. Dry camping would be best near the church.

Be careful to follow the correct, waymarked, path as you leave the pass and roughly contour on this old path until you reach the ruins of La Quera (3hr 35min). The waymarks lead you between the buildings, then fork left up a track and fork left again to regain the path. Follow the ancient path on a slowly descending traverse, with a few ups as well, of the steep SE ridge of Puig de Sant Marc (1327m), often seeming to cling to the rock face. There is a final descent to **Sant Aniol d'Aguja** (4hr 20min, 460m, N42°19.010 E002°35.272). Water-point. No camping.

Sant Aniol d'Aguja is the remains of a Benedictine monastery which was established in the 9th century and is very popular with tourists. Restoration was starting in 2013. The stream just below is good for cooling off in hot weather.

Take the path left of the church down to the **Riera de Sant Aniol**, cross the bridge and follow the path on the other side. There are lots of sideturns so watch the waymarks carefully. After 5min there are grassy clearings on your right which would make good campsites. Continue to a signed path junction. ▶ If you have some spare time it is worth considering a trip down to Sadernes.

If you turn right you will come to a swimming hole in about 5min which is better than any on the GR11.

Sadernes has a campground with a small shop and a bar-restaurant, but no accommodation.

The Riera de Sant Aniol flows down a **dramatic limestone gorge**, which is the main reason so many tourists walk up to Sant Aniol from Sadernes (70min down, 85min up without pack).

Swimming hole on Riera de Sant Aniol

Turn left, signed to Albanyà (4hr 30min), and then turn right across the **Torrent de la Comella**, after which the path climbs steadily to a viewpoint (5hr 10min). After a short respite you continue climbing to **Coll Roig** (5hr 40min, 840m, N42°18.886 E002°36.727). The first dry camping opportunity since the meadows after Sant Aniol d'Aguja. The path contours ENE from Coll Roig before climbing and then descending to a (dry) streambed (5hr 55min). Climb up to a new track at a ruin and turn right (no waymarks). Turn right at a junction and fork right down a path (6hr 10min). Cross a (dry) streambed and turn right along a track before forking left off it. Climb to a grassy area with some ruins. The path may not be clear, but it stays left of both grassy area and ruins and climbs steeply to a dirt road (6hr 45min). Turn right and soon reach **Coll de Principi** (6hr 50min, 1126m, N42°19.111 E002°38.159). Start descending on a dirt road and almost immediately fork left. The right fork is for the ascent of Puig de Bassegoda. Continue to the **Coll de Bassegoda** (6hr 55min, 1105m). Good dry camping.

Ascent of Puig de Bassegoda

Puig de Bassegoda (1374m) to the SW is your last chance to climb a 'mountain' on the GR11. Either follow the track from the Coll de Principi or a (yellow) waymarked path from the Coll de Bassegoda which soon joins the track. Continue to the track end (10min). Excellent dry campsites. Head straight up the hill on a path marked by cairns and green waymarks. Ignore paths going to the right. The final climb is an easy scramble up a limestone buttress with the aid of iron rungs (35min up, 25min down). There are magnificent views to the remainder of the GR11 and the Mediterranean to the NW in France as well as back to the high mountains.

Veer right at the pass, ignore some spurious paths and then turn sharp left after 250m. Follow a well-marked path which switchbacks steeply down through the wood to the **Refugi de Bassegoda** (7hr 25min, 820m).

> This large unmanned refuge is maintained in good condition but is kept locked to avoid vandalism. There is no water supply. Keys can be obtained, for a small fee, from Can Nou, about 5min ahead.

The GR11 now roughly contours to **Can Nou** and goes round the right-hand side of the farmhouse (7hr 30min, 780m) to its entrance at the bottom.

Can Nou has a bar-restaurant.

Follow the dirt road E from Can Nou past an old fountain. This spring was running in August 2013, but dry in 2003 and 2012. When you reach a concrete road (7hr 35min), turn left and follow it all the way to Albanyà. There are some 'shortcuts', with yellow waymarks, which you could take across some of the switchbacks if you like steep slippery paths. Eventually reach a junction at the bottom of the hill (8hr 55min). ▶

Turn right for the GR11 and follow the road downstream to **Bassegoda Park** campground (9hr 10min).

Bassegoda Park campground, with cabins as well as camping, is about 1km W of Albanyà. It has a bar-restaurant and a small supermarket which stocks 'original' and 'easy-clic' camping gas.

Puig d'en Coll from Coll Roig

It is worth turning left to find a magnificent swimming hole in La Muga a few minutes upstream, where a concrete ramp leads down to the river.

Continue down the road to GR11 noticeboard in **Albanyà** (9hr 20min, 237m, N42°18.319 E002°43.189).

Albanyà is a small village with a bar-restaurant, a small, but well stocked shop, hidden behind the church, and a couple of Casa Rural (listed below), both about 1km E of the village. The shop stocks 'original' camping gas. The Font de l'Olla is also behind the church.

Facilities on Stage 40
Càmping Masia Sadernes: tel 972 687 536 www.sadernes.com
Bassegoda Park campground: tel 972 542 020 www.bassegodapark.com
Can Carreras: tel 620 33 58 62 www.cancarreras.com
Can Mas Albanyà: tel 972 542 023 www.canmasalbanya.com

STAGE 41
Albanyà to Maçanet de Cabrenys

Start	Albanyà
Distance	21km
Total Ascent	1100m
Total Descent	1000m
Difficulty	Easy. Waymarking is just about adequate.
Time	4hr 25min
High Point	E ridge, Puig de la Trilla (690m)

The GR11 continues through steep wooded hills.

After visiting Albanyà return to the GR11 noticeboard. Continue E down a narrow concrete road, the Cami de Maçanet, with water-point. Immediately after the last house, before the bridge, turn left up a track. When the track veers right, fork left up a path (10min) and climb steeply to a track junction (25min). Take the track that goes diagonally right

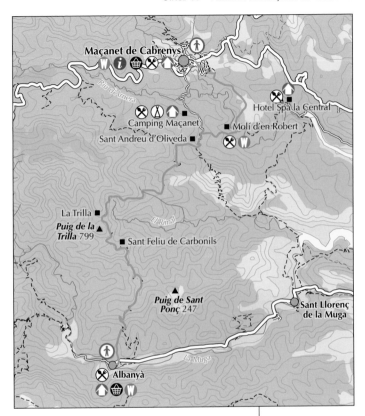

uphill and after a couple of minutes fork right up a path, shortcutting the track. On rejoining the track, turn right and immediately left for the next shortcut. Then it's left along the track, forking right to reach a junction as you reach the ridge (50min, 566m, N42°19.208 E002°43.553). Turn right and follow the track to pass an ornate gate (1hr 5min). Fork left soon after this and left again (1hr 15min) to reach a junction signed 'Carbonils' (1hr 30min). The Església de Sant Feliu de Carbonils is on your right. This is as good a place as any for a dry camp and there is an open arch round the back that might be used for a bivouac.

The GR11 keeps straight on and follows the main track, ignoring a number of sideturns, as it passes right of Puig de la Trilla to reach a grassy area. Dry camping possible. Pass the abandoned farm buildings at **La Trilla** (1hr 55min) and, at a switchback, keep straight on (ENE) along a path. Cross a (dry) streambed (2hr 5min), climb a ridge and descend to another (dry) streambed (2hr 30min). Five minutes later reach a small hilltop. Camping possible.

Pass a ruined farm, where the path becomes a track and drop down to a larger track. Turn left, then shortly afterwards, fork right and then turn left SSW along a path. This path soon veers steeply downhill to cross a woodland stream with dubious quality water (2hr 50min). Follow the path as it descends above the left-hand bank to reach a rough track. When this track veers right, fork left up a faint path (3hr) and climb steeply to a dirt road. Turn right and reach a junction, signed to Sant Andreu d'Oliveda (3hr 10min). Turn right and soon go straight across a six-way junction. Fork left along the main dirt road and left again to join a tarmac road by some expensive-looking villas (3hr 25min). Follow the road and soon reach a junction.

Camping Maçanet de Cabrenys (cabins, bar-restaurant and camping) is about 1km along the tarmac road and then you could follow the road a further 3km to Maçanet de Cabrenys.

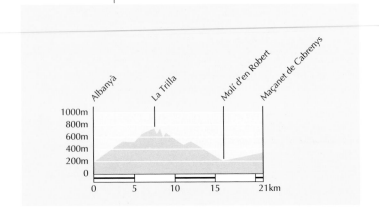

Feature from tile display in Maçanet de Cabrenys

Turn right down the dirt road for the GR11, ignoring the sign to Maçanet de Cabrenys. Cross a stream with rock pools as you reach the **Restaurant Molí d'en Robert**, which has a swimming pool (3hr 45min). Water, but no camping.

Turn right along a track after the final building. This track leads to Hotel Spa la Central, but the GR11 takes an immediate left turn up a path which climbs onto a plateau. Keep straight on along the middle track at a track junction (4hr 15min) then turn left at a junction and follow the dirt road, ignoring lots of sideturns. This becomes a tarmac road at the edge of **Maçanet de Cabrenys** (4hr 20min). A waymarked route takes you through the outskirts and across a bridge to a junction with the 'main' road (GI-503) (4hr 25min).

> Maçanet de Cabrenys is a large village with a tourist information office, three hotels, casa rural, bar-restaurants and several small shops. You pass a water-point, Font del Carrer Llarg, as you head into the village.

STAGE 42
Maçanet de Cabrenys to La Jonquera

Start	Maçanet de Cabrenys
Distance	20km
Total Ascent	600m
Total Descent	800m
Difficulty	Easy. Well waymarked as far as La Vajol, after which waymarking is limited but sufficient.
Time	4hr 50min
High Point	Puig de la Creu (600m)

The GR11 goes ENE along the 'main' road to a picnic area and GR11 information board at the edge of the village. Fork left up a track and, when the main track goes left, keep straight on along a rough track. Descend through a bouldery cork forest to a (possibly dry) stream and climb the other side. If you lose the waymarks keep going in the same direction until you reach the road to La Vajol (20min). Turn left up the road and then right along a track. The next section is well waymarked although tricky to describe. Eventually pass a small spring-fed pipe, which you may hear rather than see since it could be hidden in vegetation (40min). Water. Turn right at the next junction to reach the main road.

Turn left across the bridge and shortly afterwards turn sharp left up a path (50min, 285m, N42°23.316 E002°46.905). Fork right and climb steeply. As you near the top of the hill you reach a small track (1hr 15min). Turn right,

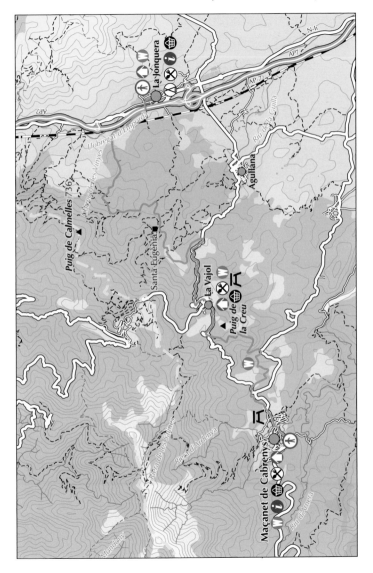

Statue at the picnic area, La Vajol

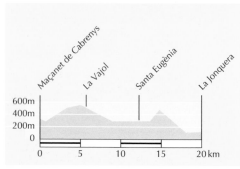

then left and then fork right, skirting W of the summit of Puig de la Creu. This track takes you to a large building above the Canta Mine (1hr 40min) where you fork right to a road (1hr 45min, 521m, N42°24.222 E002°47.353). Turn right and follow the road to a picnic site just above **La Vajol** (1hr 50min). Water-point.

> La Vajol is a small village. The Ca la Conxita bar-restaurant has a small shop for provisions and offers accommodation. The alberg (hostel), which offers basic accommodation, is open from 6pm.

Continue down the road through the hamlet. The alberg is on the right in the basement of the Ajuntment building just before Ca la Conxita bar-restaurant. You pass a water-point with many monuments, mainly commemorating the Spanish Civil War.

Continue to reach the car park at the bottom of La Vajol and follow the main road (GI-501) down for about 3.5km, ignoring lots of left turns until a dirt road goes off sharp left signed to Santa Eugenia (2hr 35min). Turn left along this dirt road. There's an area just before Mas Barell where you could camp and more camping ahead. The dirt road becomes a tarmac road for a bit and then you reach an area that appeared to be devastated by a big fire in July 2012. ▶

Continue along the road to **Santa Eugènia** (3hr 15min, 350m) which now seems to be a youth or community centre.

Most environments would have taken years or even decades to recover from a fire of this severity, but the cork-trees seem to have survived and were already recovering in 2013.

Cork pile

Take the track heading E, then fork left by a field (3hr 20min) and follow the track uphill (N). Veer sharp right (3hr 40min) and continue climbing to a track on the right (3hr 50min). Turn right and immediately left, ignoring several side-turns, before turning right at a junction with signpost (4hr 5min). Turn right alongside a fence at a junction at the bottom of the hill (4hr 25min), veering left and following the track under the railway. Rather than go over the motorway, turn right and eventually left through a tunnel under the motorway to arrive at **La Jonquera** (4hr 45min, 110m, N42°25.180 E002°52.271). Go straight on, cross the river and turn right down the 'high street', Carrer Major, until a small square, Placa de l'Ajuntament, is reached (4hr 50min).

La Jonquera is a border town with a lot of large supermarkets to serve cross-border traffic, as well as many smaller shops, hotels, bar-restaurants and two campgrounds. The author was able to find 'original' and 'easy-clic' camping gas in Sol Jonquera Supermercado and Stop Centre Commercial. There is a ferreteria in town which will probably stock camping gas, but it is closed on Sundays.

Facilities on Stage 42
Ca la Conxita: tel 972 535 213 www.calaconxita.com
The Alberg, La Vajol: tel 692 069 135 or 650 797 614.
La Jonquera Tourist Office: tel 972 545 079
Hotel Tramuntana: tel 972 554 663 www.hoteltramuntana.com
Hotel Frontera: tel 972 554 849 www.hotelfrontera.es
Font del Pla Hotel Restaurant: tel 972 556 393 www.fontdelpla.net
Hotel La Jonquera: tel 972 556 555 www.lajonquerahotel.com
AS Hoteles Porta Catalana: tel 972 554 640 www.ashotelportacatalana.com
Càmping Moli de Vent: tel 972 554 066
Camping Sant Jaume de Canadal: tel 972 555 681

STAGE 43

La Jonquera to Els Vilars

Start	La Jonquera
Distance	23km
Total Ascent	1200m
Total Descent	1100m
Difficulty	Easy and well waymarked
Time	6hr 25min
High Point	Puig dels Falguers (778m), Coll de la Llosarda (690m)

This is another difficult section for hikers who require manned accommodation. There is unlikely to be any en route accommodation between La Jonquera and Llança on the coast. Stage 43 ends at Els Vilars where there are no facilities apart from a water-point. This is where walkers requiring accommodation will need to divert from the GR11, on the alternative route described in Stage 44, to find accommodation in Espolla or Rabós. There is a bothy just after Requesens. There are camping opportunities throughout the section, but don't set your standards too high.

From the Placa de l'Ajuntament turn left up an alleyway, Carrer Sant Miquel, then first right and first left up Carrer Migdia. Veer right up Carrer Rosselló and fork left up a track. Fork left again and, at the end at the end of fenced properties, turn left up a path (10min). Turn left along a small track to join a bigger track. Fork right on a sharp left bend, then fork left and rejoin the main track. Keep straight on up a path when the track veers left (30min) and keep straight on when the path rejoins the track at a junction. Fork right at the next junction and almost immediately fork left up a path (40min). Turn left up a track, and then fork left on a path when the track starts descending (55min) to arrive at a picnic table and good water-point, Font de la Soula (1hr).

Climb steps to **Ermita de Santa Llúcia** with a covered shelter, suitable for a bivouac. The hermitage, main picnic site, another shelter and a fine viewpoint are on your right. The GR11 follows waymarks up a path to the left. This sometimes rough or eroded path climbs steadily through the

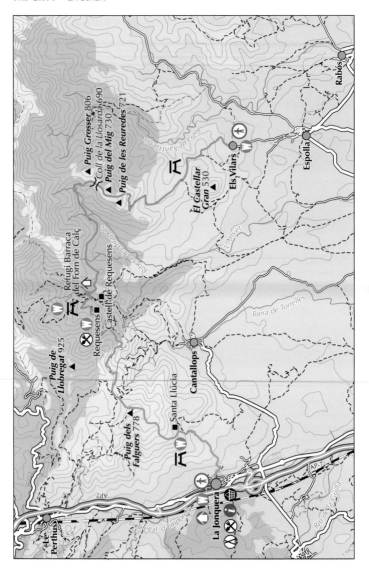

*Fire damage above
Ermita de Santa Llúcia*

area which was most devastated by the 2012 fire, eventually reaching a col (2hr). Continue up the ridge to cross the summit plateau of **Puig dels Falguers** (2hr 10min, 778m, N42°26.384 E002°54.150).

The GR11 now leaves the fire-damaged area and continues roughly NE along a small path, crosses a grassy col and continues over rocky terrain to a track junction (2hr 25min). Turn right along a major track. Five minutes later you should see above you the remains, actually most of the plane, of a DC 6 which crashed into the trees in 1986. A short distance further on a plaque on the right commemorates the French aircrew who lost their lives in the crash. Continue along the

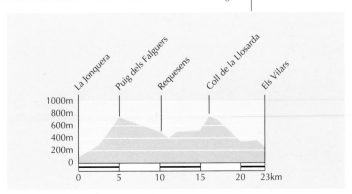

track, passing a water-point on the left on your approach to the bar-restaurant at **Requesens** (3hr 15min, 500m).

Follow the track N, soon passing a fountain with a picnic table but with dubious quality water. At the next switchback go straight on, signed to Els Vilars (3hr 25min). Cross a trickling stream and fork right, then bear left at a junction before switchbacking right as you cross another woodland stream. Soon fork left and then turn left when you meet a wall. You soon pass the **Refugi Barraca del Forn de Calç**, a small bothy which was in excellent condition in 2013 (3hr 40min, 474m). No water. Veer right then fork left and follow this track, which twists and turns. Cross another trickling woodland stream and eventually pass left of the ruins of Mas Mirapols (4hr 10min).

In a few minutes cross a woodland stream, then climb steadily and cross a trickling woodland stream (4hr 40min). Take the path that veers right from here. When a ridge is reached (4hr 55min) the path veers left and climbs a little way up the ridge before contouring right, signed to Vilamaniscle. You soon reach the open SW ridge of Puig Grosser (806m) at **Coll de la Llosarda** (5hr, 690m, N42°26.826 E002°58.999).

Mas Mirapols

Contour right of Puig del Mig (730m), cross the fence at the next saddle and contour left of Puig de les Reuredes (721m) before descending through the woods to a track (5hr 15min). Turn right and switchback down, ignoring any sideturns, passing the almost certainly dry Font de la Verna, which has a picnic table (5hr 55min). Continue to a junction as you approach **Els Vilars** and turn right to reach the hamlet (6hr 25min, 220m, N42°24.625 E002°59.827). The water-point is along the track at the bottom of the hamlet.

If you are looking for accommodation you will need to take the alternative route described in Stage 44.

STAGE 44
Els Vilars to Llançà

Distance	26km; alternative route: 19km
Total Ascent	700m; alternative route: 400m
Total Descent	1000m; alternative route: 700m
Difficulty	Easy; the alternative route via Espolla or Rabós is also easy, but there is no waymarking as it is not a recognised route.
Time	5hr 35min; alternative route: 4hr 10min
High Point	Coll de la Plaja (395m), Coll de la Serra (260m), Coll de les Portes (230m),
Note	Walkers requiring accommodation or other facilities will need to divert from the GR11 to Espolla and Rabós. Accommodation is limited, so it would be sensible to phone in advance to check on vacancies.

The approach to the Mediterranean is through hot dry hills with too much road walking.

As the track turns right on the northern edge of the Els Vilars, follow an indistinct path left. The path goes right of a dry stream, crosses it then veers right along a wall before crossing the stream again.

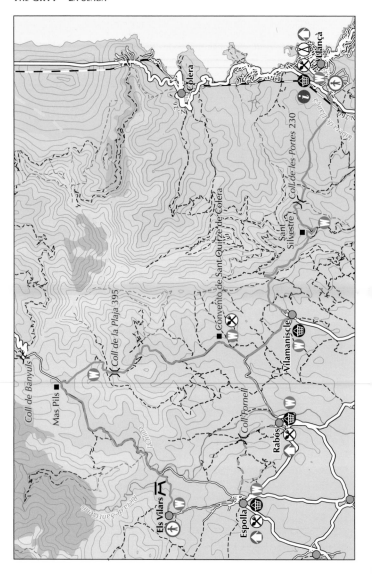

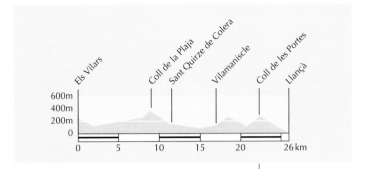

The author saw the endangered **Hermann's Tortoise** plopping into a pool in this stream. The Albera Natural Reserve is the only place on the Iberian Peninsula where this turtle survives in its natural environment.

A clear path descends the left-hand side of the (dry) stream, forking left to reach Font de Cadecàs with picnic table but probably no water (15min). Fork left up the track and soon cross a stream but its water would need serious treating before drinking. In 2012/3 the owner of the house by the stream was putting out bottles of drinking water for hikers. Reach a tarmac road (25min) and turn left along it, steadily climbing, passing Mas Corbera (Bausstiges) before reaching the ruins of **Mas Pils** on your left (1hr 30min, 250m, N42°26.376 E003°02.699).

Shortcut

If you are running out of time it would be possible to continue straight on here, crossing into France over the Coll de Banyuls and dropping down to the Mediterranean at Banyuls sur Mer, which is on the French rail network.

Turn right down a track, cross a (dry) stream. Good dry campsites. Continue until a path goes off right when the track bends left (1hr 50min). Climb the possibly overgrown path to Fonteta II and up to Fonteta I. Water-points. Turn right when you regain the track to arrive at the **Coll de la Plaja** (2hr 5min, 395m, N42°25.621 E003°02.955). Keep straight

Convento de Sant Quirze de Colera

The church dates back to at least the 9th century. There was extensive restoration being carried out on the monastery in 2013.

on until a footpath shortcuts left (2hr 15min), going straight across the track when you meet it again, then turning right along it to reach the **Convento de Sant Quirze de Colera** (2hr 25min, 165m). ◄ There is a bar-restaurant just up the track on the left, open until 5pm, but closed Wednesdays. There is a water-point, behind the convent.

Follow the dirt road, soon to become a tarmac road, to a road junction (3hr 10min). The alternative route via Espolla rejoins from the right. The GR11 goes left, passing through vineyards to reach a water-point, Font de l'Ou, with seating area and GR11 information board, as you arrive in **Vilamaniscle** (3hr 30min, 155m, N42°22.529 E003°03.970).

Vilamaniscle has very limited facilities for walkers. There are two Casa Rural (Casa Rural Cal Sisco and Caj Rajoler) but they both concentrate on weekly bookings during the holiday season. There is a small shop and the swimming pool has a bar. There is a bivouac area below the swimming pool.

Turn left at the water-point and climb steeply before turning right along Carrer Tramuntano, passing the Font del

Suro and then pass the Cases de Colonies Tramuntano, a youth camp, at the top of the village (3hr 40min). The road now becomes a dirt road which is followed to the Coll de la Serra (3hr 55min, 260m, N42°22.753 E003°04.852). Turn left, then, at the second switchback, keep straight on down a smaller track and contour along this track. As the track eventually starts descending, a path goes off left (4hr 20min) and drops steeply down to the **Església de Sant Silvestre de Valleta** (4hr 25min). ▶

The chapel dates back to the 10th century.

Follow the dirt road down from the chapel. After a couple of minutes pass the Font del Xac, just across the (dry) streambed on your right. This spring was running well in August 2012 but was only trickling in 2013. Continue to a junction with a concrete track then turn sharp left. This track gradually veers right as it climbs through abandoned terraces to reach the **Coll de les Portes** (4hr 55min, 230m, N42°22.248 E003°06.549). Keep straight on to the next col (5hr) where the descent to **Llançà** begins. Follow the track to pass under the railway (5hr 30min) on the outskirts of town. Turn left after the bridge along a very broad dirt road to arrive at the main road. Cross the road to Llançà Tourist Office

Església de Sant Silvestre

(5hr 35min, 15m, N42°21.754 E003°08.846). There is big supermarket on your right. There is a water-point in the park behind the tourist office.

> Llançà has all the facilities you would expect of a seaside tourist resort, with a wide range of accommodation which could be fully booked in high season. At the cheaper end of the market you could try Alberg Costa Brava (beside the railway station), Hab. Pacreu, Pensió Llançà or Càmping l'Ombra.

Alternative route via Espolla and Rabós

Distances rather than times are given as the author researched the route by bicycle.

◄ If you need accommodation, leave the GR11 and follow the track through Els Vilars. There is a water-point at the bottom of the hamlet where you join a tarmac road and follow it S to **Espolla** (2.2km). Fork left of the church and then turn right, round the edge of the village, to just before a rough parking area (2.6km). Turn right for Can Salas and other facilities in Espolla.

> Espolla has a Turisme Rural, Can Salas, several small shops and bar-restaurants.

Otherwise turn left (E) along a concrete track, signed to Rabós and Vilamaniscle. Ignore lots of minor tracks and eventually the track becomes a dirt track (3.6km). Continue along the 'main' track, pass a concrete 'drive' to a house on a ridge and reach a four-way junction under electricity wires at **Col Fornell** (4.6km). Turn right and follow the track, which becomes a concrete track just before you fork right

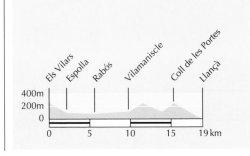

down a tarmac road to arrive at **Rabós** by the bar-restaurant (5.7km).

> Rabós has several Casa Rural (including Casa Rural Can Puig, Casa Rabós and El Paller de l'Albera), a bar-restaurant and a small supermarket.

Fork left at the 'square' and drop down to a bridge at the E edge of the hamlet (6km). There is a water-point just before the bridge. Turn left along a tarmac road, signed to Vilamaniscle to reach a road junction (8.2km, about 1hr 45min) where you rejoin the GR11 to Vilamaniscle and Llançà (about 4hr 10min).

Facilities on Stage 44
Can Salas: tel 972 563 376
Casa Rural Can Puig: tel 972 563 092 www.canpuig.net
Casa Rabós: tel 972 563 903 www.casarabos.es
El Paller de l'Albera (website says minimum 2 nights): tel 661 489 595
    www.elpaller-rabos.com
Casa Rural Cal Sisco: tel 932 093 593
Caj Rajoler: tel 972 853 291 www.canrajoler.com
Alberg Costa Brava: tel 972 380 384 www.albergcostabrava.com
Hab. Pacreu: tel 972 380 337
Pensió Llançà: tel 972 380 119 www.pensionllanca.com
Camping l'Ombra: tel 972 380 335 www.camping-lombra-llanca.com
Llançà Tourist Information Office: tel 972 380 855 www.llanca.net

STAGE 45
Llançà to Cap de Creus

Start	Llançà
Distance	27km
Total Ascent/Descent	1100m
Difficulty	Easy
Time	7hr 25min
High Point	Sant Pere de Rodes (500m)
Note	There is only very limited accommodation at Cap de Creus and no water-point, so you need to decide what to do when you get there. It might be better to divide this section into two so you arrive at Cap de Creus in the afternoon. There are places for discrete camping throughout the route.

There is a 'sting in the tail', with a 500m climb to Sant Pere de Rodes before descending to el Port de la Selva, followed by a path through dry scrub to the peninsula of Cap de Creus on the Mediterranean Sea.

This wide road was built for development which has been halted by the crash in the construction industry.

Go left of the tourist office then veer right, keeping the park on your right, and turn left past some flats, following signs to Coll de Perer. ◄ Fork right up a small track from the roundabout at the top of the road (10min). Ignore a right turn as the track joins an old walled path (25min) and continue to a path junction on the **Coll del Perer** (1hr 5min, 356m). Turn right and climb to the **Serra de l'Estella** ridge (1hr 25min, 462m, N42°20.426 E003°09.231). Turn left along a track, forking left to reach a road junction. Keep straight on along the middle road, signed to St. Pere de Rodes, passing the Església de Santa Elena to arrive at the popular tourist attraction of the **Monasterio de Sant Pere de Rodes** (2hr, 500m).

The first authenticated mention of the **monastery** site dates from 878 when there was a simple monastic cell dedicated to St. Peter. By 945 this had developed into a Benedictine monastery, which reached its peak in the 11th and 12th centuries when it

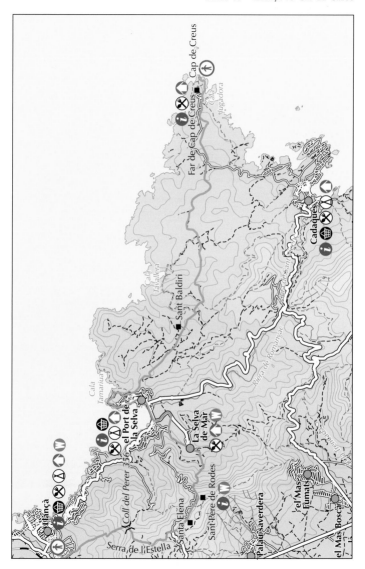

251

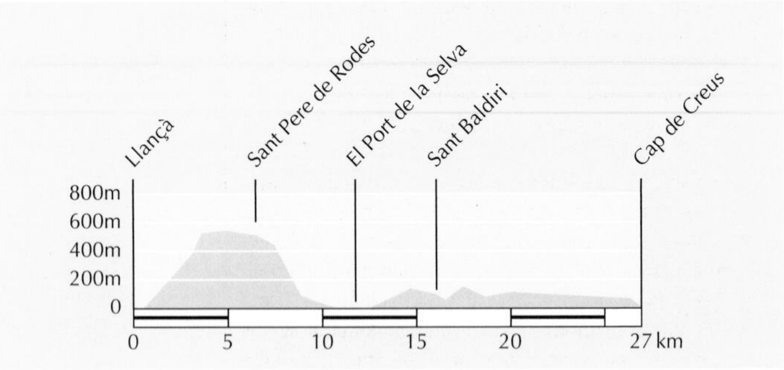
Llançà
Sant Pere de Rodes
El Port de la Selva
Sant Baldiri
Cap de Creus
800m
600m
400m
200m
0
0
5
10
15
20
27 km

became an important point of pilgrimage. The monastery declined in the 17th century before being abandoned in 1793. It was declared a National Monument in 1930 with restoration starting in 1935.

Follow the concrete track forking down left, immediately left of the monastery. Almost immediately pass a waterpoint on a terrace on your left. Follow the concrete track to a car park (2hr 5min). Fork right down a path from the car park and descend steeply to reach a track (2hr 35min). Follow the path straight across this this track and descend left of a dry

Sant Pere de Rhodes

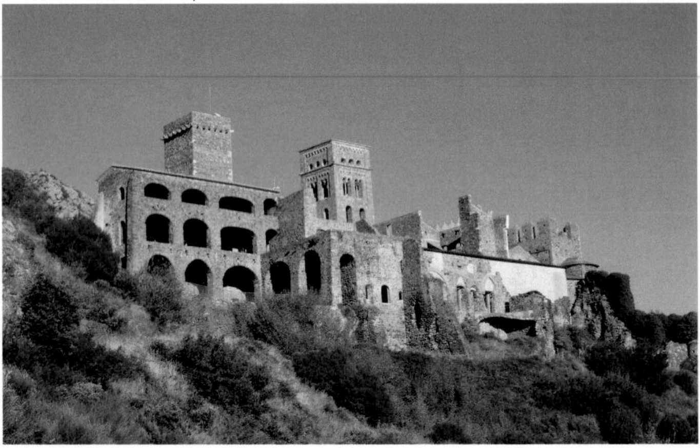

gully to reach the Eglésia de Sant Sebastià. Pass right of the chapel to enter **La Selva de Mar**.

> La Selva de Mar is a hamlet with a bar-restaurant (Fonda Felip) which offers accommodation.

Turn along the left-hand side of the (dry) stream and pass a water-point, Font Mollor. Turn right across a bridge and immediately left. Then turn left down an alley and right along the stream. Cross the stream and follow a small path along the left-hand bank. Fork left along a track then left up a path which climbs to another track. Turn right and follow this track to the road descending from Sant Pere. Stay right of the barrier and descend right on a path, then left along a track to reach the GI-6121 road. Turn left along the path beside the road to reach **El Port de la Selva** by Hostal l'Arola. Turn right and follow the GR11 along the seafront to reach the main beach (3hr 20min). Water-points and beach showers.

> El Port de la Selva has all the facilities you would expect of a seaside tourist resort, including three campgrounds (listed below) and a wide choice of accommodation. It will be very busy in high season.

Follow the road along the seafront and above the small beaches to the N of the town. When the coast road starts descending to Cala Tamariua – with its small sandy beach where bathing costumes are optional – fork right, signed to Cap de Creus, to a high point on the road (3hr 55min, 85m, N42°20.345 E003°12.469). Follow a track going off left and ignore a turning to the ruins of Mas Puignau (4hr 20min). Shortly afterwards turn right at a junction and then second left, keeping straight on when the main track switchbacks. Keep straight on at a complex junction to arrive at the remains of **Sant Baldiri de Taballera** (4hr 30min).

The track now veers right as a path and after a few twists and turns follows a wall, before forking right across the wall, descending into a dry valley and climbing out the other side, passing to the S of Mas Paltré. ▶

The GR11 crosses the track and follows another heading roughly E. Pass the ruins of Mas Vell and fork right. A little later a path veers left into another dry valley and climbs out the other side. At the top, among a number of stone structures

You could turn left here and follow this track to Cala Tavallera, which has a super little beach. Camping might be possible here. Climb the obvious path to the SW of the beach to return to the GR11.

just right of the trail is a stone shelter which would serve for an emergency bivouac (5hr 20min). There are a number of other stone shelters, but they look even more uncomfortable. After a few minutes you fork left down a path, left along a track, then fork right keeping a close eye on the waymarks and eventually pass a ruined farmhouse and then an abandoned farmhouse. Keep straight on (slightly left) along a minor track and soon approach the road to Cap de Creus, but the GR11 continues a bit further as a path before crossing the road (6hr 30min, 100m, N42°19.088 E003°17.536). The GR11 continues right of the road, occasionally just touching it. The well-waymarked path follows a complex route which takes you close to **Cala Jugadora**, which has a small sandy beach, before reaching the **lighthouse** (7hr 10min). From here follow GR waymarks (or local path 15) to the **Punta de Cap de Creus** where the terminus of the GR11 is marked by a rather insignificant cairn (7hr 25min, N42°19.159 E003°19.311). It is a short scramble down to the Mediterranean Sea.

Small beach at Cala Jugadora

The lighthouse at Cap de Creus has a café (open 10am–9pm in the main holiday season) and tourist

Surf at Cap de Creus

information office and toilets. There is no water-point. Bar-restaurant Cap de Creus, which is adjacent to the lighthouse, also offers expensive accommodation and late-night entertainment.

Cadaqués, to the SW of Cap de Creus, is a well-developed tourist resort with about 25 hotels and a campground.

Facilities on Stage 45
Fonda Felip: tel 972 387 271
El Port de la Selva Tourist Information Office: tel 972 387 122
    www.elportdelaselva.cat
Hostal and Camping l'Arola: tel 972 387 005
Camping Port de la Selva: tel 972 387 287 www.campingselva.com
Camping Port Valley (static caravans as well as camping): tel 972 387 186
    www.campingportdelavall.com
Hostal La Tina: tel 972 387 149 www.hostallatina.cat
Hotel-Restaurant Cal Mariner: tel 972 388 005 www.calmariner.com
Bar-restaurant Cap de Creus: tel 972 199 005 http://restaurantcapdecreus.
    blogspot.co.uk
Cadaqués Tourist Information Office: tel 972 258 315 www.visitcadaques.org

APPENDIX A
Route summary table

Stage	Distance (km)	Total ascent (m)	Total descent (m)	Time (hr:min)	Cumulative distance (km)	Cumulative time (hr)
1 Cabo de Higuer – Bera	30	1100	1100	8:05	30	8
2 Bera – Elizondo	31	1400	1200	7:40	61	16
3 Elizondo – Puerto de Urkiago	19	1100	400	5:30	80	21
4 Puerto de Urkiago – Burguete	18	800	800	4:55	98	26
5 Burguete – Hiriberri	18	600	600	4:45	116	31
6 Hiriberri – Ochagavía	21	800	1000	5:55	137	37
7 Ochagavía – Isaba	20	700	700	5:05	157	42
8 Isaba – Zuriza (GR11-4)	17	1400	1000	6:50	174	49
9 Zuriza – La Mina	12	800	800	3:50	186	53
9A Zuriza – Puen de Santana	22	1100	1400	6:35		
10 La Mina – Candanchú (GR 11)	22	900	600	6:30	208	59
10A Puen de Santana – Ref. de Lizara (GR11-1)	12	1200	500	4:50		
10B Ref. de Lizara – Candanchú (alt route)	17	800	800	6:00		
11 Candanchú – Sallent de Gállego (GR11)	23	900	1200	6:35	231	66
12 Sallent de Gállego – Ref. de Respomuso	12	900	100	3:50	243	70
13 Ref. de Respomuso – Baños de Panticosa	13	700	1300	6:10	256	76
14 Baños de Panticosa – San N. de Bujaruelo	21	1100	1400	7:05	277	83
15 San Nicolás de Bujaruelo – Ref. de Góriz	24	1600	800	7:35	301	90
16 Ref. de Góriz – Ref. de Pineto (GR11)	13	1000	2000	6:50	324	97
17 Ref. de Pineto – Parzán	21	1000	1200	6:05	345	103
18 Parzán – Ref. de Biadós	22	1500	900	6:10	367	110
19 Ref. de Biadós – Puen de San Chaime	21	1000	1500	6:25	388	116
20 Puen de San Chaime – Ref. de Cap de Llauset	18	1700	400	6:20	406	122
21 Ref. de Cap de Llauset – Ref. de Conangles	11	200	1100	3:30	417	126

Stage	Distance (km)	Total ascent (m)	Total descent (m)	Time (hr:min)	Cumulative distance (km)	Cumulative time (hr)
22 Ref. de Conangles – Ref. dera Restanca	13	1100	600	5:00	430	131
23 Ref. dera Restanca – Ref. dera Colomèrs (GR11-18)	8	700	600	3:30	438	134
24 Ref. de Colomèrs – Espot	18	500	1300	5:50	456	140
25 Espot – La Guingueta d'Àneu	10	200	600	2:25	466	142
26 La Guingueta d'Àneu – Estaon	10	1400	1100	5:10	476	148
27 Estaon – Tavascan	12	1000	1200	3:50	488	151
28 Tavascan – Àreu	16	1800	1600	6:10	504	158
29 Àreu – Ref. de Vallferrera	9	900	200	3:15	513	161
30 Ref. de Vallferrera – Ref. de Comapedrosa	10	900	500	5:05	523	165
31 Ref. de Comapedrosa – Arans	9	500	1400	3:50	532	169
32 Arans – Encamp	12	1200	1300	5:20	544	174
33 Encamp – Ref. de l'Illa	15	1500	300	5:25	559	181
33A Encamp–Ref. Cap del Rec (GR11-10)	25	1800	1000	8:20		
34 Ref. de l'Illa – Ref. de Malniu	14	1000	1300	5:15	573	186
34A Ref. Cap del Rec – Ref. Malniu (GR11-10)	21	1500	1300	7:35		
35 Ref. de Malniu – Puigcerdà	14	100	1100	3:10	587	189
36 Puigcerdà – Camping Can Fosses	25	1200	1100	6:25	612	195
37 Camping Can Fosses, Planoles – Núria	18	1600	900	5:55	630	201
38 Núria – Setcases	19	1100	1800	5:50	649	207
39 Setcases – Beget	21	1100	1800	6:20	670	213
40 Beget – Albanyà	31	2200	2500	9:20	701	223
41 Albanyà – Maçanet de Cabrenys	21	1100	1000	4:25	722	227
42 Maçanet de Cabrenys – La Jonquera	20	600	800	4:50	742	232
43 La Jonquera – Els Vilars	23	1200	1100	6:25	765	238
44 Els Vilars – Llançà (GR11)	26	700	1000	5:35	791	244
44A Els Vilars – Llançà (via Espolla)	19	400	700	4:10		
45 Llançà – Cap de Creus	27	1100	1100	7:25	818	251
Total	**818**	**46,000**	**46,000**	**251**		

APPENDIX B

Facilities table

Stage no	Place	Hotel/hostel	Manned refuge	Bothy	Camp-ground	Bar-restaurant	Food shop	Tourist office
1	Cabo de Higuer				✓	✓		
	Hondarribia	✓			✓	✓	✓	
	Irún	✓				✓	✓	✓
	Ermita San Martzial					✓		
	Embalse de San Antón					✓		
	Bera	✓				✓	✓	✓
2	Collado de Lizarrieta					✓	✓	
	Elizondo	✓				✓	✓	✓
3	Puerto de Urkiaga							
4	Albergue Sorogain	✓				✓		
	Burguete	✓			✓	✓	✓	
5	Orbara					✓		
	Hiriberri	✓				✓		
6	Paso de Las Alforjas			✓				
	Ochagavía	✓			✓	✓	✓	✓
7	Zotrapea			✓				
	Isaba	✓				✓	✓	✓
8	Zuriza	✓			✓	✓	✓	
9	La Mina							
9A	Puen de Santana	✓				✓		
10	Achar d'Aguas Tuertas			✓				
	Puerto de Somport (alt route)	✓				✓		
	Candanchú	✓	✓			✓	✓	✓
10A	Above Puen de Santana	✓	✓		✓	✓		
	Refugio de Lizara		✓			✓		
10B	Above Refugio de Lizara			✓				
	Barranco de Bernera			✓				
11	below Candanchú			✓				

Stage no	Place	Hotel/hostel	Manned refuge	Bothy	Camp-ground	Bar-restaurant	Food shop	Tourist office
	Canal Roya			✓				
	Río Gállego			✓		✓		
	Sallent de Gállego	✓			✓	✓	✓	
12	Embalse de la Serra					✓		✓
	Refugio de Respomuso		✓			✓		
13	Ibón Baxo de Bachimaña		✓			✓		
	Baños de Panticosa	✓	✓			✓		
14	Río Ara			✓				
	San Nicolás de Bujaruelo		✓		✓	✓		
15	Camping Valle de Bujaruelo	✓			✓	✓	✓	
	Torla (off route)	✓			✓	✓	✓	
	Ordesa Canyon					✓		✓
	Refugio de Góriz		✓		✓	✓	✓	✓
16	Refugio de Pineto		✓			✓		
17	Ermita de Pineta	✓				✓		
	Plana es Corders			✓				✓
	Parzán	✓				✓	✓	
18	Barranco d'Ordizeto			✓				
	Collata Chistau			✓				
	Refugio de Lisiert			✓				
	Es Plans				✓	✓		
	Refugio de Biadós		✓			✓		
19	Pleta d'Añes Cruces			✓				
	Refugio d'Estós		✓			✓		
	on the descent to Puen de San Chaime			✓				
	Puen de San Chaime	✓			✓	✓	✓	
	Benasque (off route)	✓			✓	✓	✓	✓
19A + 19B	Refugio d'Ángel Orús		✓			✓		
20	Barranco de Ballibierna			✓				

Stage no	Place	Hotel/ hostel	Manned refuge	Bothy	Camp-ground	Bar-restaurant	Food shop	Tourist office
	Refugio Cap de Llauset	tbc				tbc		
21	Refugio d'Angliós			✓				
	Refugi de Conangles		✓			✓		
22	Refugi dera Restanca		✓			✓		
23 (GR11.18)	Refugi de Colomèrs		✓			✓		
23 (GR11)	Ribera de Rius			✓				
24	Refugi d'Amitges (off-route)		✓			✓		
	Estany de Sant Maurici		✓	✓		✓		✓
	Espot	✓			✓	✓	✓	
25	Ríu Escrita				✓	✓	✓	
	La Guingueta d'Àneu	✓			✓	✓	✓	
26	Estaon		✓			✓		
27	Tavascan	✓				✓	✓	✓
28	Àreu	✓			✓	✓	✓	
29	Refugi de Vallferrera		✓			✓		
30	Refugi de Baiau			✓				
	Refugi de Comapedrosa		✓			✓		
31	Arinsal	✓				✓	✓	
	Arans	✓				✓		
32	Ordino (off route)	✓			✓	✓	✓	✓
	Encamp	✓			✓	✓	✓	✓
33	Riu Madriu			✓				
	Refugio de l'Illa			✓				
33A + 34A	Refugi de Perafita			✓				
	Refugi Estanys de la Pera		✓			✓		
	Refugi Cap del Rec		✓			✓		
	Viliella					✓		
34	Cabana dels Esparvers			✓				
	Refugi Engorgs			✓				
	Refugi de Malniu		✓			✓		

Stage no	Place	Hotel/ hostel	Manned refuge	Bothy	Camp- ground	Bar- restaurant	Food shop	Tourist office
35	Refugi de la Feixa			✓				
	Guils de Cerdánya					✓		
	East of Saneja				✓	✓	✓	
	Puigcerdà	✓				✓	✓	✓
36	Age	✓						
	Planoles	✓			✓	✓	✓	
37	Refugi Corral Blanc		✓			✓		
	Queralbs	✓				✓	✓	
	Núria	✓			✓	✓	✓	✓
38	Refugi d'Ulldeter		✓			✓		
	Hostal Pastuira	✓				✓		
	Setcases	✓				✓	✓	
39	Molló	✓				✓	✓	
	Beget	✓				✓		
40	Refugi de Bassegoda			✓				
	Can Nou					✓		
	Albanyà	✓			✓	✓	✓	
41	Camping Maçanet de Cabrenys (off route)				✓	✓		
	Maçanet de Cabrenys	✓				✓	✓	✓
42	La Vajol	✓				✓	✓	
	La Jonquera	✓			✓	✓	✓	✓
43	Requesens			✓		✓		
	Els Vilars							
44	Sant Quirze de Colera					✓		
	Vilamaniscle						✓	
	Llançà	✓			✓	✓	✓	✓
44A	Espolla (alternative route)	✓				✓	✓	
	Rabós	✓				✓	✓	
45	La Selva de Mar	✓				✓		
	El Port de la Selva	✓			✓	✓	✓	✓
	Cap de Creus	✓				✓		✓

APPENDIX C
Glossary

A = Aragón B = Basque C = Catalan

Spanish	English
Abri	cabin
Achar (A)	narrow pass
Agua	water
Aguja	needle
Alt, Alto	high
Arroyo	stream
Avenida	avenue
Avinguda (C)	avenue
Azul	blue
Baix, Baxo	low
Balle (A)	valley
Balneario	thermal baths
Biskar (B)	shoulder
Borda	farm
Bosc (C)	wood
Bosque	wood
Brecha	gap
Caballo	horse
Cabana	cabin
Cabezo	small hill
Cabo	cape
Cala (C)	small bay
Calle	street
Calm (C)	bare plateau
Camino	track
Campo	meadow

Spanish	English
Can (C)	house
Canal	narrow valley
Cap	small hill
Capella	chapel
Carrer (C)	street
Carretera	road
Casa	house
Cascada	waterfall
Caserio	farm
Castillo	castle
Circo	coombe
Col, Coll (C)	pass
Colladeta	small pass
Collado	pass
Coma (A)	coombe
Creu (C)	cross
Cuello (A)	pass
Embalse	reservoir
Entibo (A)	reservoir
Ermita	hermitage
Espelunga (A)	cave
Estacion	station
Estany, Estanh (C)	
Estiba (A)	summer pasture
Fábrica	factory
Faro	lighthouse

Spanish	English
Feixa (C)	ledge
Font (C)	spring
Fronton (B)	pelota wall
Fuén (A)	spring
Fuente	spring
Gran	large
Hospital	Inn
Hostal	small hotel
Ibón (A)	lake
Iturri (B)	spring
Lac (A), Lago	lake
Llano	flat area
Mas (C)	farmhouse
Mendi, Monte	mountain
Monasterio	monastery
Muga (A, B)	frontier stone
Negre	black
Nord	north
Obago (C)	dark
Orri	stone shelter
Paso	pass
Pena (A)	crag
Pic (C)	peak
Pica (C), Pico	peak
Pista	track
Pla (C)	flat area
Placa	town square
Plan (A)	flat area
Pont (A, C)	bridge
Port (C)	pass
Portella	small pass

Spanish	English
Prado	meadow
Puen (A)	bridge
Puente	bridge
Puerto	pass
Puig (C)	peak
Refugi (C)	mountain hut
Refugio	mountain hut
Regata	stream
Río, Riu (C)	river
San, Sant (C)	saint
Santa	saint
Sanctuario	sanctuary
Serra (C)	mountain range
Sobira (C)	high
Soum	rounded mountain
Sud	south
Torrente	mountain stream
Tuc (C)	sharp summit
Tuca (A, C)	sharp summit
Val (A), Valle	valley
Vall (C)	valley

APPENDIX D
Sources of information

Maps

The cheapest way to get a complete detailed map of the GR11 is to buy the Spanish Guide, GR11 Senda Pirenaica, produced by Prames. This guide comes complete with 46 map pages at 1:40,000. At the time of writing these maps are being updated and are accurate at the western end of the Pyrenees but are rather inaccurate at the eastern end.

The best maps are those of Editorial Alpina at scales varying from 1:25,000 to 1:50,000.

Maps Worldwide Ltd
15 Evans Business Centre
Hampton Park Road
Melksham
Wilts
SN12 6LH
www.mapsworldwide.com

The Map Shop
15 High Street
Upton-upon-Severn
Worcs
WR8 0HJ
www.themapshop.co.uk
themapshop@btinternet.com

Edward Stanford Ltd
12–14 Long Acre
London
WC2E 9LP
www.stanfords.co.uk
sales@stanfords.co.uk

Cordee Ltd
www.cordee.co.uk
sales@cordee.co.uk

Bibliography

Other Cicerone guides to the Pyrenees (www.cicerone.co.uk):

Pyrenean Haute Route
by Ton Joosten (2012)

The GR10 Trail by Paul Lucia (2013

Walks and Climbs in the Pyrenees
by Kev Reynolds (2010)

The Mountains of Andorra
by Alf Robertson and Jane Meadowcroft (2005)

The Pyrenees by Kev Reynolds (2010)

Interesting journals/blogs on the GR11

Brian Johnson's account of his 2003 traverse of the GR11:
www.trailjournals.com/entry.cfm?trailname=4166

http://uncaminoquetecagas.blogspot.co.uk/2007_09_02_archive.html

http://gr11blog.blogspot.co.uk

www.davidgilbert.org.uk/GR11/GR11index.html

Information on mountain refuges

Information and booking for albergues, manned and unmanned refuges in Aragón:

www.fam.es

www.alberguesyrefugiosdearagon.com

Information and booking for refuges in Catalonia:
http://feec.cat
tel 934 120 777

For tourist information and information on refuges in Andorra:
http://visitandorra.com/en/home

Travel information

Brittany Ferries
www.brittany-ferries.co.uk

National Express coaches
www.nationalexpress.com

Eurolines coaches
www.eurolines.co.uk

Rail Europe
www.raileurope.co.uk

Eurostar
www.eurostar.com

French rail network
www.voyages-sncf.co.uk

French SNCF bus connections
www.ter-sncf.com

Spanish rail network
www.renfe.com

RyanAir
www.ryanair.com

British Airways
www.britishairways.com

Air France
www.airfrance.co.uk

Easyjet
www.easyjet.com

Telephone codes

Europe-wide emergency telephone number: 112

International telephone codes

UK 44 (0044 UK from Spain)

France 33 (0033 from UK)

Spain 34 (0034 from UK)

Andorra 376 (00376 from UK)

Weather forecasts for the Pyrenees

www.hikepyrenees.co.uk/pyrenees-weather-forecast.html

www.mountain-forecast.com

Descent from Puerto de Chistau (Stage 19)

Sat 2nd July - Taxi 3.30am

Flight GTW South 06:20

Arr Biaritz 09:05

Booked : Hotel Restaurant Santiago (Hendaye - paid)

Sun 3rd : Walk Irun - Bera

Stay @ Hostal Auzoa (not paid)

4th   Walk Bera - Elizondo
        Stay @ Kortarixar

5th   Walk Elizondo - ~~Auberge~~ Albergue Saroquin (booked)

6th   Walk to Burguete (taxi to Pamplona)

Stay @ AC Hotel Zizur Mayor.

The Great Outdoors

DIGITAL EDITIONS
30-DAY
FREE TRIAL

- Substantial savings on the newsstand price and print subscriptions
- Instant access wherever you are, even if you are offline
- Back issues at your fingertips

Downloading **The Great Outdoors** to your digital device is easy, just follow the steps below:

1 **Download the App** from the App Store

2 **Open the App**, click on 'subscriptions' and choose an annual subscription

3 **Download** the latest issue and enjoy

The digital edition is also available on

The 30-day free trial is not available on Android or Pocketmags and is only available to new subscribers

LISTING OF CICERONE GUIDES

Trekking in the Vosges and Jura
Vanoise Ski Touring
Via Ferratas of the French Alps
Walking in the Auvergne
Walking in the Cathar Region
Walking in the Cevennes
Walking in the Dordogne
Walking in the Haute Savoie
North & South
Walking in the Languedoc
Walking in the Tarentaise and
Beaufortain Alps
Walking on Corsica

GERMANY

Germany's Romantic Road
Hiking and Biking in the
Black Forest
Walking in the Bavarian Alps
Walking the River Rhine Trail

HIMALAYA

Annapurna
Bhutan
Everest
Garhwal and Kumaon
Kangchenjunga
Langtang with Gosainkund
and Helambu
Manaslu
The Mount Kailash Trek
Trekking in Ladakh
Trekking in the Himalaya

ICELAND & GREENLAND

Trekking in Greenland
Walking and Trekking in Iceland

IRELAND

Irish Coastal Walks
The Irish Coast to Coast Walk
The Mountains of Ireland

ITALY

Gran Paradiso
Sibillini National Park
Stelvio National Park
Shorter Walks in the Dolomites
Through the Italian Alps
Trekking in the Apennines
Trekking in the Dolomites
Via Ferratas of the Italian
Dolomites: Vols 1 & 2
Walking in Abruzzo
Walking in Sardinia

Walking in Sicily
Walking in the Central
Italian Alps
Walking in the Dolomites
Walking in Tuscany
Walking on the Amalfi Coast
Walking the Italian Lakes

MEDITERRANEAN

Jordan – Walks, Treks, Caves,
Climbs and Canyons
The Ala Dag
The High Mountains of Crete
The Mountains of Greece
Treks and Climbs in Wadi Rum
Walking in Malta
Western Crete

NORTH AMERICA

British Columbia
The Grand Canyon
The John Muir Trail
The Pacific Crest Trail

SOUTH AMERICA

Aconcagua and the
Southern Andes
Hiking and Biking Peru's
Inca Trails
Torres del Paine

SCANDINAVIA

Walking in Norway

SLOVENIA, CROATIA AND MONTENEGRO

The Julian Alps of Slovenia
The Mountains of Montenegro
Trekking in Slovenia
Walking in Croatia
Walking in Slovenia:
The Karavanke

SPAIN AND PORTUGAL

Costa Blanca: West
Mountain Walking in
Southern Catalunya
The Mountains of Central Spain
The Northern Caminos
Trekking through Mallorca
Walking in Madeira
Walking in Mallorca
Walking in Menorca
Walking in the Algarve
Walking in the Cordillera
Cantabrica

Walking in the Sierra Nevada
Walking on Gran Canaria
Walking on La Gomera and
El Hierro
Walking on La Palma
Walking on Tenerife
Walking the GR7 in Andalucia
Walks and Climbs in the
Picos de Europa

SWITZERLAND

Alpine Pass Route
Canyoning in the Alps
Central Switzerland
The Bernese Alps
The Swiss Alps
Tour of the Jungfrau Region
Walking in the Valais
Walking in Ticino
Walks in the Engadine

TECHNIQUES

Geocaching in the UK
Indoor Climbing
Lightweight Camping
Map and Compass
Mountain Weather
Moveable Feasts
Outdoor Photography
Polar Exploration
Rock Climbing
Sport Climbing
The Book of the Bivvy
The Hillwalker's Guide to
Mountaineering
The Hillwalker's Manual

MINI GUIDES

Alpine Flowers
Avalanche!
Navigating with a GPS
Navigation
Pocket First Aid and
Wilderness Medicine
Snow

MOUNTAIN LITERATURE

8000m
A Walk in the Clouds
Unjustifiable Risk?

For full information on all our
guides, and to order books and
eBooks, visit our website:
www.cicerone.co.uk.

Walking – Trekking – Mountaineering – Climbing – Cycling

Over 40 years, Cicerone have built up an outstanding collection of 300 guides, inspiring all sorts of amazing adventures.

Every guide comes from extensive exploration and research by our expert authors, all with a passion for their subjects. They are frequently praised, endorsed and used by clubs, instructors and outdoor organisations.

All our titles can now be bought as **e-books** and many as iPad and Kindle files and we will continue to make all our guides available for these and many other devices.

Our website shows any **new information** we've received since a book was published. Please do let us know if you find anything has changed, so that we can pass on the latest details. On our **website** you'll also find some great ideas and lots of information, including sample chapters, contents lists, reviews, articles and a photo gallery.

It's easy to keep in touch with what's going on at Cicerone, by getting our monthly **free e-newsletter**, which is full of offers, competitions, up-to-date information and topical articles. You can subscribe on our home page and also follow us on **Facebook** and **Twitter**, as well as our **blog**.

Cicerone – the very best guides for exploring the world.

CICERONE

2 Police Square Milnthorpe Cumbria LA7 7PY
Tel: 015395 62069 info@cicerone.co.uk
www.cicerone.co.uk